RICHARD III

A SMALL GUIDE TO
THE GREAT DEBATE

RICHARD III

A SMALL GUIDE TO
THE GREAT DEBATE

ANNETTE CARSON

Imprimis
Imprimatur

Also by Annette Carson:

Flight Unlimited (with Eric Müller)
Flight Unlimited '95 (with Eric Müller)
Flight Fantastic: The Illustrated History of Aerobatics
Jeff Beck: Crazy Fingers
Richard III: The Maligned King

Published by Imprimis Imprimatur
21 Havergate, Horstead, NR12 7EJ
email@annettecarson.plus.com

British Library Cataloguing in Publication Data.
A catalogue record for this book is available from the British Library.

ISBN 978-0-9576840-0-3

Printed/bound in England by Barnwell Print, Dunkirk, Aylsham, NR11 6SU

Contents

*Richard III, facial reconstruction based on
his remains recovered from the Greyfriars Church, Leicester,
commissioned by the Richard III Society, 2013*

1
RICHARD III TODAY

The recent dramatic discovery of Richard III's grave in Leicester gave rise to enormous media interest. The media were interested because of the huge and ongoing fascination of the general public with Richard III, both the man and the legend.

Fame feeds on itself. Newspapers and magazines were duly brimming over with articles, most of them reproducing the usual stories by the usual people who made up their minds about Richard years ago (newspapers seldom commission original research) ... and naturally they were peppered with quotations and pictures from Shakespeare's play.

The television screen loves Richard because as a visual medium it can choose from myriads of vivid images to depict him. Plus of course there's never any shortage of people delighted to give their opinion on air, usually in the context of some overall theme or series, pronouncing their view on the person they imagine Richard III to have been. Yet Ricardian scholars are rarely given airtime to discuss the real, historical Richard, and as I write this, no seriously researched biographical documentary has ever been made.

Probably it's considered that the introduction of sober facts would diminish the sensational aura that surrounds Richard III. The vocabulary is always dramatic, the presenters and scene-setting are studiedly theatrical, edgy, angled, playing to a chosen audience. A good example of this is the potted history presented by the tour guides at the Tower of London.

This raises an interesting question. Do we prefer our history as a series of easily digested statements, neatly pigeonholed? This king was bad/ruthless/tyrannical, this other king was ineffectual, another was challenged by his barons, another won wars, another carried out religious persecutions?

Alternatively, if history is more nuanced than this, should it be left to the professors and their academic research? Is it too dry and dusty to be enjoyable – or comprehensible – unless sexed-up or dumbed-down for popular consumption?

On the contrary, I think that the stories of past lives in past centuries are exciting, relevant and enlightening. Equally enlightening is to revisit what previous generations have made of our common history, and to discover those many truths that were unknown to past researchers.

One thing I cannot emphasize strongly enough when dealing with history: it's vital to avoid 'looking back', you have to put yourself firmly in the past as if it is the present. We must be willing to do this just as we do with fiction – which is not easy, since only a few non-fiction history books have the gift of bringing to life the strangely foreign world their characters inhabit.

Richard's world was a feudal system in which rank, especially royal rank, commanded obedience. The vast majority of those who were ruled had the obligation to respect their betters, observe the laws and conventions, fight when conscripted, pray when expected, and remain dutiful and loyal to their masters.

The ruling classes had obligations in turn, and all things were governed by the king with advice from his council. Those who chose to play the Great Game of power, seeking to manipulate, challenge or overthrow their rulers, knew how dangerous a pursuit it was, with perilous outcomes (and often the axe) for those who lost.

When looking at the king himself it is vital to suspend moral sensibilities about the absolute power vested in mediaeval monarchy, where a king's person was the human embodiment of the realm, its people, its security and defence, its justice, its entire social order. Many traditional historians seem to sit in judgement on the autocratic rights of royalty five centuries ago, implying that they should (and could) conform to standards of ordinary mortals in more recent eras. This is not to discredit historians. But if each new generation fails to question its predecessors, then received wisdom will simply become solidified into orthodoxy, and fresh insights will be seen as heresy.

This is why I consistently emphasize two things when writing about Richard III: that we actually *don't* know as much as we're led to *think* we know; and that it's down to each of us to make up our own minds, not just believe what we're told (by anyone, including me!).

Unless you have read his diary – and unfortunately we didn't find one buried with him – it's necessary to face the fact that there will be a lot of unanswered questions. Almost everything we've been told about Richard III is hearsay, much of it unreliable. Richard's reign may seem very familiar thanks to the lurid stories we've all heard, but these were told by writers of later generations employing the sudden new mushrooming of printing and publishing. During his lifetime no one wrote literature dramatizing the bloody exploits of previous kings and praising present ones. There were no theatres where playwrights could parade such characters on stage as heroes or villains, personified in flesh and blood by actors.

The Tudors are so much a part of our 'Merrie England' tradition that it's forgotten how they seized the throne over the bodies of thousands of English dead in a French-backed invasion. They had a lot to answer for, and one way of justifying their actions was to pretend that Richard was hated by his people because of his many crimes. They couldn't discredit his good governance, since sources including the Bishop of St David's and the City Council of York indicate that his methods were admired, and even half a century later his laws were praised by Henry VIII's House of Commons.

However, what the Tudors could do was vilify him personally, and in this they had the incredible luck to benefit from that new printing technology which, greatest of all ironies, Richard III himself had made laws to encourage.

To understand how this was facilitated, let me draw a parallel with William the Conqueror who mounted a triumphant propaganda campaign which was adopted by the chroniclers, undermining and vilifying England's chosen king Harold Godwinson (Harold II), and after killing him set about eliminating all opposition. Interestingly, one of his moves was to brand those faithful to Harold as traitors on the grounds that they had supported a 'usurper', thus rendering their possessions liable to confiscation by William. Henry Tudor (Henry VII) would play precisely the same hand after killing Richard III.

So King Harold was denigrated in the 1060s, to the profit of his enemies, just as King Richard was in the 1480s. We have precious few records telling Harold's side of the story, because it was only after he lost his life and his throne that his reputation needed defending – and by then his supporters were silenced. For the same reason we will look in vain for records from Richard's reign telling his side of the story. Unlike his successor, he didn't live long enough to commission historians to write books talking up his virtues.

There is, in any case, a significant overall lack of narrative material from the period before printing took off. Usually we look for monkish chronicles which typically act as useful sources for what little we know of the Middle Ages. But we have only one from Richard's reign, and its contents were written from the standpoint of his opponents – with no counterbalancing chronicle written from a supporting angle, or at least none that survived the Tudor era and the Dissolution of the Monasteries.

When academics over the last five centuries have set down their judgements and conclusions, they have usually accepted the Tudor interpretations of the few clues that exist, just as the Norman characterization of Harold Godwinson was accepted until scholars delved deeper into pre-Norman England. Knowing that history is written by the winners, these neatly packaged constructions ought not to be taken at face value. Where Richard III is concerned, we are dealing with an amalgam of deduction, surmise, conjecture and cynicism, viewed through the propaganda of Richard's enemies, and topped off with a fantasy figure invented by Shakespeare.

If we are to take the standpoint of 'innocent until proved guilty' we need to question those assumptions, and we may find ourselves without easy answers.

I would rather be candid about this, uncomfortable though it may be for anyone who prefers ready made certainties. What I'm hoping is that you will share with me the fascination of the detection process involved in teasing out a few nuggets of truth from a giant edifice of gossip, rumour and speculation. I may not provide you with answers myself, but I hope my questions may lead you to reach your own informed opinions.

* * *

At this point I should declare an interest: I am not an academic historian but a professional non-fiction writer, mainly concentrating on historical, biographical and technical subjects. My last book was entitled *Richard III: The Maligned King*, so it should be evident where my sympathies lie.

I was not at the outset a Ricardian, but had been aware of the Great Debate since my school days, and the book was an attempt to weigh up the arguments. Even now I find them difficult to pin down, owing to the irksome lack of reliable evidence. But on balance I have found myself unwilling to condemn a man where reliable evidence of the case against him is so signally lacking, and generally depends on adopting the most jaundiced view whenever there is ambiguity.

Having carried out exhaustive research on a topic which obviously fascinates people from all corners of the world, I think the arguments are best served by being set out frankly and approached with an open mind.

If after reading this *Small Guide* you feel desirous of finding out more for yourself, my book *The Maligned King* contains a handy Appendix where the principal sources are listed, with their recommended current editions, most of which are available in libraries and online. My invariable advice in relation to Richard III is always to go back to the 15th century and read the sources for yourself. There is also a Richard III Society which has enormous resources, an informative website, and branches around the world with their own websites offering downloadable information.

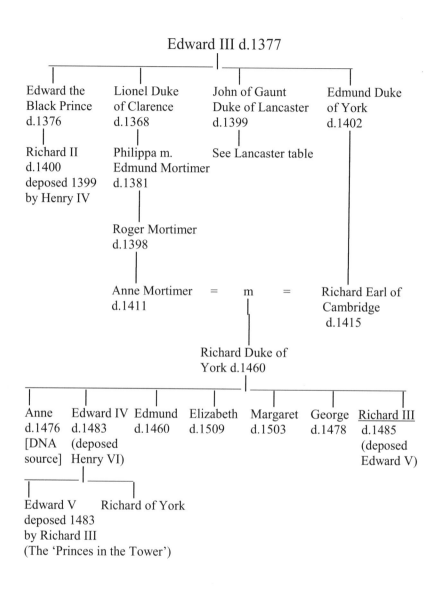

Edward III d.1377

Edward the Black Prince d.1376

Richard II d.1400 deposed 1399 by Henry IV

Lionel Duke of Clarence d.1368

Philippa m. Edmund Mortimer d.1381

Roger Mortimer d.1398

Anne Mortimer d.1411   =   m   =   Richard Earl of Cambridge d.1415

John of Gaunt Duke of Lancaster d.1399

See Lancaster table

Edmund Duke of York d.1402

Richard Duke of York d.1460

Anne d.1476 [DNA source]

Edward IV d.1483 (deposed Henry VI)

Edmund d.1460

Elizabeth d.1509

Margaret d.1503

George d.1478

Richard III d.1485 (deposed Edward V)

Edward V deposed 1483 by Richard III (The 'Princes in the Tower')

Richard of York

House of York family tree (simplified)

2
WHO WAS THE REAL RICHARD III?

To view a member of the mediaeval nobility in the context of his time you need to slot him into his place in a society which was divided roughly into 'those who work', 'those who pray', and 'those who fight'. The primary duty of the nobility, from the king down-wards, was the feudal responsibility to bear arms and to preserve the realm from threats, both external and internal.

It is extremely difficult to build an accurate profile of any person from the distant past, especially a 15th-century duke or king – but the starting point has to be his rank and role in life.

By the time his detractors had finished with Richard he was a deformed, hobbling hunchbacked monster with a string of murders to his name, whose good actions were sheer hypocrisy, and whose high reputation for valour was merely the mark of an effective killing machine. This summary is not an exaggeration, and the charges of 'hypocrite' and 'hatchet-man' have pursued him into the 21st century.

The problem is how to find the human being underneath it all, without wandering off into equally unacceptable realms of supposition. For this brief thumbnail sketch I will try to stick to facts verifiable in records dating from the time of his reign.

From what we know of him, Richard was a conscientious and conventional member of his class, in an age when the ties that bound them were those of *good lordship* to their retainers and supporters, *oath-swearing* to their superiors, and *fides publica*, loyalty to the state.

Among their preferred reading matter would be books of chivalry and military strategy such as Richard owned. His father, the Duke of York, had a lengthy military career and Richard himself was sent as a young boy to receive a military and courtly education in the Yorkshire household of the Earl of Warwick at Middleham castle.

Born on 2 October 1452, Richard was not to enjoy a life of ease even though his father was a royal duke. By the time he was nine he'd already had many frightening and disastrous experiences due to the armed hostilities between his extended family and other noble houses. He had spent time as a captive and fugitive, and knew hardship and loss culminating in the death of a father and a brother. But then suddenly within a few months had come the accession of his eldest brother as King Edward IV and his own elevation to Duke of Gloucester.

Such an elevation brought problems of its own. Richard was certainly not brought up as a pampered prince at a royal court, and like most younger sons he had no personal inheritance. Edward IV had two younger brothers and both needed financial provision, supplied mainly by means of confiscations from wrongdoers and asset-stripping from their families (Edward also asset-stripped from his own supporters when it suited him).

Edward's rule did not go uncontested. From age 16 to 18 Richard found himself supporting his brother through sporadic uprisings, battles, and a flight to safety into Flanders.

After a few months Edward retrieved the throne again, by which time Richard had distinguished himself in the field and led the vanguard in the final, decisive battle of Tewkesbury (May 1471). He would remain Edward IV's foremost general for the rest of his brother's life. In a poem of praise he was addressed as:

The Duke of Gloucester, that noble prince,
Young of age and victorious in battle,
To the honour of Hector that he might come,
Grace him followeth, fortune and good speed.

By the age of 17 Richard was already Edward's right-hand man, the very image of the king's prop and loyal support, a position recognized in his appointment as High Constable of England for life.

King Edward IV
Richard III's eldest brother

This appointment placed him at England's heraldic and chivalric pinnacle. It made him responsible for the Law of Arms on behalf of the crown in his own summary court, the Court of Chivalry (or Constable's Court), where he judged and delivered sentence in cases of armed insurrection and treason.

This career of military and public service may sound quite unremarkable, but it was a model of devotion by comparison with the feuds and intrigues frequently carried on within European ruling families. Edward entrusted Richard with offices and powers 'for his nearness and fidelity of relationship … for his proved skill in military matters and his other virtues'. Such dignities were not bestowed upon the third of the three surviving York brothers, George Duke of Clarence, despite being Richard's elder by three years.

George coveted his brother's crown and, ever hopeful of gaining it, whipped up rebellion against him. When Edward IV eventually tried and executed George for treason, Richard was said to have been overcome with grief. It was a cruel lesson in the awesome necessity for a king to preserve his person and protect his throne.

Of Richard's personal interests we know that he owned a number of books, several of them well-thumbed, among which were books of religion. This, together with his many religious endowments, has convinced historians that he was genuinely pious. He was renowned for his love of music, and was known to have sent around the country seeking to recruit gifted musicians to his service.

His intelligence has been deduced from many evidences, including the large proportion of Latin books in his possession, even the quality of his handwriting. Actually all three brothers were renowned for their intelligence, like their father before them. When a legal dispute arose between the brothers, it was commented that 'all who stood around, even those learned in law, marvelled at the profusion of their arguments'.

On a more intimate level, we know a little of Richard's marriage with the widowed Lady Anne Neville, the younger of the Earl of Warwick's two daughters, whom he had probably known as a child when he had undergone chivalric training in her father's household.

A tragic conflict of loyalties had arisen when Warwick rebelled against King Edward. He had persuaded George to join him, marry his elder daughter Isabel, and stand a chance of taking the crown for himself. When this first rebellion failed, Warwick then cemented an alliance with the defeated house of Lancaster by giving the hand of his younger daughter, 14-year-old Anne, in marriage to the former Lancastrian Prince of Wales (son of Henry VI) in return for his partnership in another attempt. This also ended in disaster.

Before her 15th birthday Anne's father was dead and she was left widowed and defenceless. George meanwhile had reconciled with his family, and as Anne's brother-in-law he appointed himself her guardian. His wife and Anne were co-heiresses of a huge inheritance, and his plan was to control Anne's share as well as Isabel's. Knowing that Richard hoped to marry Anne, George tried everything within his power to prevent the marriage. He went to the extraordinary lengths of taking Anne to London where he hid her away disguised as a kitchen worker. But Richard eventually found her, placed her in sanctuary, and won her hand as well as the king's approval of the match.

They remained married for around 13 years, most of them spent together at her late father's castle at Middleham. But Anne appears not to have been strong. She produced only one surviving child, a little boy who died aged about eight, and she herself died, possibly of tuberculosis, in early 1485.

During these years Richard had been established as Edward IV's viceroy in the turbulent North of England. He gained a solid reputation taking care of the troubled northern parts and border country, and it was reported that he won loyalty and 'the favour of the people' for his justice and fair dealing.

* * *

On gaining the throne after Edward's death, Richard made clear his determination to promote justice under the law for everyone, something that in previous reigns had been open to the highest bidder or whoever was best equipped to intimidate juries and witnesses.

One of his most famous actions was to call together all the justices and put them on the spot with a number of searching questions. He ended by giving them a clear rule he expected them to live up to: 'To say "by my justices" and to say "by my law" is to say one and the same thing.' This was not at all how things worked in an age where court decisions could be bought by bribery and influence.

In his Parliament he introduced a number of legal reforms which benefited ordinary people. For the first time he ensured that only men of good character and property-owners could serve on juries. He established a system of bail to protect suspected offenders from lengthy imprisonment before trial, when previously suspects could be imprisoned indefinitely and have their assets raided: Richard made it illegal to seize a person's property before he was convicted. He made enactments designed to curb sharp practices, e.g. by standardizing weights and measures, and by introducing published title to property – this prevented the same property from being repeatedly sold by unscrupulous owners.

Among his other reforms he developed what would become known as the Court of Requests, making himself accessible to the poor who could not afford legal representation.

In a later century Sir Francis Bacon would describe Richard III as 'a good lawmaker for the ease and solace of the common people'. None of this was designed to please the men who wielded power, and it is possible that he paid a high price for it at Bosworth Field.

Once he was king, naturally any complimentary remarks about Richard III are likely to be attributable to currying favour. Some really grotesque examples have survived, showing people praising him to his face and denigrating him after his downfall. Nevertheless one such item of flattery contains a few significant words which may have been chosen to reflect Richard's known concerns for the less fortunate: 'punishing offenders of his laws, especially extortioners and oppressors of his commons ... he got great thanks of God and love of all his subjects rich and poor'.

Less likely to be flattery was a personal letter to the prior of Christ Church, Canterbury, written by the Bishop of St David's, who had watched during Richard's royal progress as he refused several rich civic gifts: 'he contents the people where he goes best that ever did prince ... Many a poor man ... has been relieved and helped by him and his commands in his progress. I never liked the condition of any prince so well as his; God hath sent him to us for the weal of us all'.

To offset the possibility that this was special pleading by someone who had done well out of the new king, it should be added that the bishop also had some caustic words to say about 'sensual pleasure' which 'holds sway to an increasing extent'. Maybe he was someone who didn't approve of lavish entertainments at court. This at least tells us Richard wasn't all about po-faced puritanism, and it chimes with his known love of music.

Another not-for-publication comment appeared in the private journal of Niclas von Popplau, a visiting knight from Silesia who was invited to spend several days in Richard's company: 'O dear God, what a great-hearted lord I recognized in the king!'

There are many small ways we can gain insights into Richard's approach to power, one of them being that he caused the law to be set out in English instead of the usual Latin and French, and had it put on public display so that everyone could understand it.

Other clues may be found in the modest grants and concessions he made to assist ordinary people. An example which still resonates was when he discharged a clerk from the Privy Seal office for obtaining his post through bribery over the heads of the under-clerks, who had, as the king remarked, 'long continued therein', having spent 'the flower of their ages' in hopes of that promotion.

Perhaps the most famous comment about Richard, which might almost serve as his epitaph, was written into the York council records when news of his death reached the city fathers, men who had known him and worked with him for years. 'King Richard, late mercifully reigning upon us … was piteously slain and murdered to the great heaviness of this city.'

The above few facts and quotations are matters of record which can readily be checked. There seems little negative comment about Richard's character written during his lifetime by anyone who actually knew him.

But there were factions who opposed his rise to power, rejected his claim to the throne, took up armed revolt and sought to remove him. And there were observers of the political scene who wrote expressing disapproval of him for this and other reasons. Their arguments lie at the heart of the controversy and need to be taken seriously, so they will be fully examined in later chapters.

But before we discuss these rational arguments, we need to penetrate the smokescreen of distortions introduced to misdirect people's perceptions during the Tudor era.

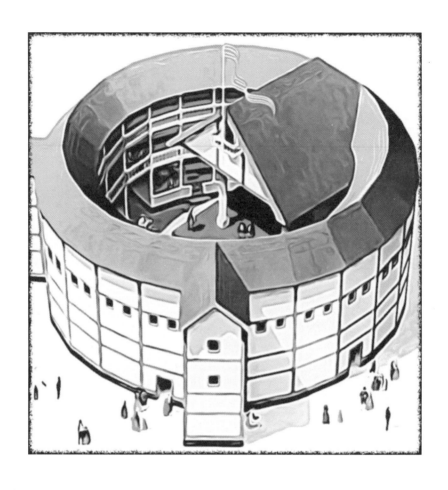

Shakespeare's play 'The Tragedy of King Richard III'
was composed for the entertainment of Elizabethan theatregoers

3
THE BLACK LEGEND

In a recent slim publication about the Tower of London by Historic Royal Palaces, the index gave thirteen references to Richard III and the 'Princes in the Tower'. The illustrations included no fewer than three depictions of a pair of terrified boys in melodramatic poses, awaiting their fate at the hands of their wicked uncle. By contrast the book yielded a mere handful of references to the murderous Henry VIII, from whom the Tower derives the bulk of its blood-soaked reputation, and no portrayals of any of his anguished victims with broken, tortured bodies awaiting the blessed relief of death on the scaffold.

As you can see from the above, emotions are not difficult to manipulate whether with words or pictures. So let us take a clear-eyed look at history stripped of the editorializing, and get to the bottom of how the black legend of Richard III came about.

In a brief little book like this I have to confine myself to the core accusations that are levelled against Richard, so I have chosen the principal two: the **usurpation of the throne**, and the **murder of the 'Princes in the Tower'**. They will have to be taken in chronological order, because the second depends upon the first.

Shakespeare's *Tragedy of King Richard III* is mainly responsible for today's public perception of Richard, so it is essential to dispose of his play before getting down to look at reality. The two accusations named above are the nucleus of his case for the prosecution, although for good measure he throws in a string of other deaths in which Richard historically had no discernible role. (Actually the list of deaths occurring in the play *Richard III* stretched back over the previous 12 years, but accuracy was never something that bothered the bard – in an earlier play he depicted the Duke of Somerset killed by Richard at the age of two!)

In Shakespeare's speeches, Richard himself makes clear his motivation for his crimes: his foul deformity. This is absolutely central to the play.

In this day and age, thankfully, we no longer think of disability as they did in the 16th century. We find terms like 'hunchback' unpleasant and distasteful, and the association of evil with deformity is unthinkable. But in Shakespeare's day a malformed body was inextricably linked with sinfulness, a sign of judgement by God. Richard's alleged deformity had been thoroughly well entrenched over the previous 100 years of Tudor rule, and in order to ensure that the attribute of a twisted body was firmly linked to that of a twisted mind, all known portraits of Richard III dating from the Tudor era were painted (or, if necessary, overpainted) to show either one shoulder higher than the other, or various disfigurements such as withered limbs, scowls, narrowed eyes, meanly clenched lips, etc. Shakespeare himself makes Richard's body an incarnation of inner wickedness by giving him a combination of hunched back, withered arm and hobbling leg.

Fortunately we now have evidence that Richard was not a 'hunchback' but had a lateral curve to his spine (scoliosis), a condition seemingly shared by quite a large number of our population even in the 21st century, including the Olympic gold medallist Usain Bolt. And we know for sure that all four of Richard's limbs were straight and sound.

These scientifically verified facts are more revelatory than they might at first seem, because they strike at the heart of the age-old question: did the Tudors speak the truth about the man they replaced on the throne, or did they blacken his name with propaganda?

The best propaganda (or 'spin' as we tend to call it today) takes a small element of fact and magnifies or distorts it into something to suit one's own argument. So, based on our investigations of Richard's remains, we can safely conclude that there was some serious Tudor spin going on.

And if we can agree to dismiss the contorted physique of Shakespeare's monstrous Richard, then we must at the same time discount the basis upon which his character's moral degeneracy hinges.

Yet it is this very image of deformity and degeneracy, usually as performed by Laurence Olivier, that is repeatedly trotted out in film clips whenever a TV item mentions Richard III. Is it surprising that Richard the extravagantly black-hearted villain is now embedded in our collective psyche?

Those constantly replayed visuals, and the air of theatricality they introduce, are incredibly difficult to get past. Yet we must attempt to set Shakespeare aside, along with all those worlds of fiction and entertainment, otherwise we shall never get to grips with the real man at the heart of the Great Debate.

* * *

As we all know, when Shakespeare was writing in the 1590s this was more than a century after Richard's death. Shakespeare did not enjoy an education of the sort that acquainted him with mediaeval English history. So when writing what are known as his 'history plays' he relied on stories written by other people. Principal among these was a collection by Raphael Holinshed. Holinshed himself copied other publications by Richard Grafton, John Rastell, Edward Hall, etc.

The remarkable background to the emergence of such books was the burgeoning age of the printing press, a revolution in information technology comparable to the arrival of the World Wide Web.

Before the age of printing all written material had to be copied out sheet by sheet, individually and laboriously, by hand. In the 15th century books grew more popular, and book production became a cottage industry, but the volumes reproduced were mainly well-established works of reference, 'improving' literature and poetry, devotional works, Books of Hours and so on, usually produced on commission. The concept of a private individual initiating copies of a self-penned book for his own amusement was extraordinarily rare.

The arrival of Caxton's printing press in England brought the technology that would usher in mass production, and by the time Richard Grafton set up his printing business around the 1540s, author-initiated book production was well under way, i.e. someone who had the means and interest to write out some tract or treatise or

chronicle, not necessarily his own, could arrange for multiple copies to be published.

These were then spread around, copied again with added errors, changes and embellishments (either the writer's own or borrowed from the words of others), and quite likely the amended result would be printed afresh under the name of some new person. Grafton himself published 'chronicles' under his own name that were clearly plagiarized from other writers.

It's important to know this free-for-all was going on, because it explains the unreliability of the popular works produced by amateur self-styled chroniclers in the 16th century which provided the material for playwrights like Shakespeare. We have no way of knowing how much information (if any) was derived from their authors' research, personal knowledge or family tradition, or from what has been called 'the exuberance of their own verbosity'.

One of the most popular of these was a *History of King Richard III* which was written by Sir Thomas More.

In view of the pedestal occupied by More in the public esteem, it was almost impossible prior to the 20th century to suggest that his *History of King Richard III* might have been anything but sober fact (despite his authorship of the fictional *Utopia*) and unvarnished truth (despite his capacity, as a lawyer, to argue a case from any required angle).

More himself never even finished it, but the enterprising Grafton got hold of a copy and tacked it on to the end of one of his 'chronicle' publications. It was an immediate hit: the dramatic story of a double-dealing, deformed monster of wickedness to whom everyone is a pawn in his ruthless lust for the crown. More, with his usual sardonic touch, even includes a scene where his Richard III plans the murder of the princes while he is on the privy (where More, incidentally, also pictured Martin Luther celebrating Mass).

Thanks to its colourful language and vivid storytelling, the contents of More's tale kept reappearing, in part or in whole, in other publications including Holinshed's.

The main problem with More's *History of King Richard III* was that it wasn't a history (or a biography), but a dramatic construction of how a tyrant named Richard III seized the crown and murdered his nephews, written at least 30 years after its subject's lifetime by someone who was five years old when this supposedly happened.

The details it contains, of secret political machinations in the highest royal circles, were so far outside its author's own experience that we have to wonder who his unnamed informants could possibly have been: 'as men say', he writes, or 'I have heard by such men', or 'as men constantly say', or 'this have I by credible information learned', etc. Since most Plantagenets had been eliminated and their supporters well and truly silenced by then, it is unlikely that any admirer of Richard III had a hand in it.

Thomas More seems to have been still tinkering with his manuscript in about the 1520s, and we can track his earliest efforts back to perhaps 1515. This is roughly the same period when a classically-trained Italian cleric named Polydore Vergil was also writing about England's history, only Polydore made a substantially more historian-like stab at it.

There are hugely varying opinions about whether More's intention was to write a parody of the self-consciously literary style of Vergil … or whether he was writing a satirical drama in the theatrical vein … or whether it was a disguised condemnation of the tyrannical rule of the late King Henry VII whom he detested but dared not criticize by name.

More had a particular loathing for tyranny, and his worst nightmares must have come true when he found himself the right-hand man of Henry's despotic son, Henry VIII (who executed him in 1535). He would have been well aware of the explosive nature of his portrait of the tyrannous king, which is probably why he had no intention of publishing it, and never mentioned a word about it in any of his writings.

Whichever way you look at it, More's *Richard III* was clearly intended as high drama, and many experts believe he was not particularly interested in factual events at all, except as a framework for the moralistic tale he set out to tell. In fact it is so full of glaring inaccuracies that you have to wonder whether he didn't deliberately scatter mistakes around, perhaps so that if he showed it to his friends, they would know it was never meant to be what it said in the title.

For example, although More's description of Richard takes a detailed inventory of his physical features ('little of stature, ill-featured in limbs, crook-backed, his left shoulder much higher than his right, hard favoured of visage …' and so on and on), yet he reverses the disparity of his shoulders. We now know that in real life Richard's right shoulder was actually the higher one – another useful new fact we have discovered, since his scoliosis isn't mentioned in physical descriptions by people who met him.

Thomas More also gets names and ages of his characters wrong, and gives Richard that withered arm we now know was fictitious. In his narrative he also invents pages of dialogue for Richard and his other main characters. So More's 'History' was certainly not what you and I know as history, despite being accepted as such by many generations of historians.

I have spent time on More in order to illustrate how the trail links him, via Grafton and many others during the Tudor publishing boom, to Rafael Holinshed and William Shakespeare. Interestingly Shakespeare, the dramatist-poet, also decided to do some reversing of his own for better effect. Whereas More wrote 'It is for truth reported' that Richard was born so late that he emerged with teeth, Shakespeare decided that his Richard's birth would be premature: 'sent before my time / Into this breathing world scarce half made up.'

* * *

Obviously a question now arises: how did it come about that Richard was a figure of evil incarnate by around 1515, with an entire catalogue of deformities already in place, both exaggerated and invented?

A clue can be found if we go back to the writings of Polydore Vergil, that Italian cleric mentioned above, whose description of Richard, though a bit more restrained, is remarkably similar to More's: 'little of stature, deformed of body, the one shoulder being higher than the other, a short and sour countenance,' etc. Vergil also reported that withered arm we now know was invented.

Around 1508 Polydore Vergil had been given a commission by King Henry VII, the man responsible for Richard III's death at Bosworth, to write a history of the English nation. Since the Italian had arrived on these shores only in 1502, this was quite a clever move by the king because Vergil would be able to write only what he gathered from other people. And Vergil had very good reason to glean his information from sources approved by King Henry.

At this time, after twenty-odd years on the throne, Henry was sick and unpopular. He would die the following year. Because he had not come to the throne by inheritance, he had no long-established royal family to buttress the succession. Worse, his eldest son Arthur, Prince of Wales, had died in 1502, leaving him only one son.

His reign had been plagued by plots and uprisings in the name of Richard III's Plantagenet dynasty, at least one army being led by a young man claiming to be one of the 'Princes in the Tower' returning to claim his crown.

Thomas More commented that some people remained in doubt, even as he was writing his *History of King Richard III*, whether the boys had been killed in Richard's reign or not. And this despite the fact that in 1502, coinciding with the death of Henry's first son, the king had (apparently) tried to scotch the idea of their survival by suddenly putting out a complete and detailed story of exactly how Richard had commissioned their murder 19 years earlier.

The word 'apparently' has been used because the sole authority for the story's origination with Henry VII is Francis Bacon's biography of that king, written in 1622. Bacon states that the king 'gave it out', although he doesn't indicate how he knows this.

Thomas More is the first and only source that relates this detailed story, saying it emanates from a confession by Richard's Master of the Horse, Sir James Tyrell. (In 1502 Tyrell was indeed examined and executed by Henry, but on a totally unrelated charge of treason.)

The tale specifies with suitable outrage precisely how Tyrell 'devised that they should be murdered in their beds' – by suffocation – having first obtained the keys of the Tower on Richard's orders, employing a cast of characters that includes a William Slaughter ('Black Will'), Miles Forest ('a fellow fleshed in murder before') and John Dighton ('a big broad square strong knave').

Thus we are told how and when the killing was done and who carried it out, with the entire cast of murderers being identified by name and/or job description and, it would seem, also by known reputation; yet despite being an officer of the London courts – he was called to the Bar in 1502 – Thomas More gives no report of attempts to bring any of the killers to justice for regicide ('Dighton yet walketh on alive', he adds helpfully).

Unless More made it all up, it is difficult to see how anyone but the king or his top enforcers could have been in a position to know (or invent) details of what they extracted from prisoners under duress. They were very good at publicizing other confessions, and you'd think this was an extremely valuable incriminating document, therefore it seems significant that neither the confession, nor any speech from the scaffold, nor any report of it other than by More and his copiers, has ever come to light. In fact, if More's *Richard III* had remained unpublished, we should never have heard that Tyrell supposedly confessed at all.

It has been mentioned that some people doubted whether the princes had been killed in Richard's day, which Henry must have known. So it was in this climate that he commissioned his full-scale history of the English people, in which he could be sure Polydore Vergil would record the approved story of Richard III's illegal reign and murder of the princes, ending with a suitably admiring section on Henry VII and his dynasty.

This was duly written down by Vergil, with plenty of moralizing about evil having been overcome by the virtuous Tudors (although Vergil too, after Henry's death, wrote of a general report and belief that the princes were still alive and 'conveyed secretly away').

When Thomas More took up his pen he was not writing about centuries of English history like Vergil, but about one individual, Richard III, his archetype of the tyrannous king based on stories he'd heard. As a literary drama it needed a good deal of imaginative padding out. So it contains lengthy dialogue and set-piece scenes of high theatricality, along with embroidery involving names, events and circumstances, and a blow-by-blow analysis of how every action of Richard's was either wicked or, if apparently benign, an exercise in studied hypocrisy. It was a chilling tale well told, and no wonder it appealed to Shakespeare.

* * *

An important point remains to be mentioned in relation to Richard's 'black legend'. There is no accumulation of comment that we can *actually date to when he was alive* to convince us that he was generally viewed by Englishmen as a tyrant or a murderer. Certainly the way he seized power aroused personal opposition – we'll come to that in chapter 5 – which naturally generated censure and dark mistrust among partisans of those affected. England was also in a state of hostility with Scotland, and in addition her ancient enemy, France, had just pulled out of a peace agreement and was renewing attempts at destabilizing the English government. So Richard was being assailed by adverse propaganda from various directions.

Yet from all the English sources set down during his reign, despite the inevitable criticism, there is no convincing evidence that Richard made tyrannous laws, extorted unjustified taxes, lined his own pocket, caused religious persecution, sowed dissent among his nobles, oppressed his commons, or killed the 'Princes in the Tower'.

In fact we know he had to subsidize the royal exchequer after the

29

death of his brother the king, and refused gifts of gold saying he would rather have the people's love. Actions that speak in his favour are many, including an admirable record of administration in the North; but they will not be recited here – we have other fish to fry.

Naturally, when relying on sources that are 'convincing', I have to exclude uncorroborated allegations from his rivals and opponents, or from hostile foreign powers who would seize any opportunity to vilify and besmirch those holding rule in England. In this connection it seems odd that so many historians have credited a defamatory statement made by the Chancellor of France to the effect that Edward IV's sons were murdered and the crown given to their murderer. This was delivered in early 1484 as part of a resounding tirade against the English and their rulers, when this French statesman could have no way of knowing whether it was true. In fact the best source of intelligence the Chancellor could have consulted, an agent named Dominic Mancini who had recently returned from England, said categorically that he knew nothing about the fate of the princes.

This was not an age when information travelled reliably, and there was no guarantee that even someone living close to the scene of events would have anything more than gossip to go on. The farther away in distance or in elapsed time, the less reliable the report.

So if we are looking for a truthful source to tell us what English people generally thought of Richard, we shall not find it in French politically motivated rhetoric, or in any of the rumours being spread on the Continent about goings-on in England.

When we try to rid ourselves of those items which were derived from unreliable or uncorroborated speculation, or which merely quoted assumptions or gossip they were in no position to verify, what do we have left?

Aside from official documents and records, books of accounts and some private notes and letters, there is one solitary narrative report from Richard's lifetime that describes some of the events as they happened in 1483 and tries to put them into perspective. This is the report from the foreign agent Mancini (another example, unfortunately, of developments in England being portrayed with an anti-English bias). There is also a narrative written shortly after his death, the anonymous native chronicle compiled by the monks of Crowland Abbey, which also contains a section on Richard's reign.

We will come to both of these in more detail below.

Otherwise the sad fact is that there's a lamentably short supply of English written sources about Richard III from his own day, and almost no personal testimony that will assist with the Great Debate; which is why generations of historians descended so happily on Tudor writers who were never reluctant to spread their thoughts around on paper. Even the king's historian Polydore Vergil remarked on the meagre amount of source material from Richard's era, something which has itself given rise to some suspicion.

What is immediately apparent, however, is that a string of allegations started to be levelled against Richard III in England as soon as he was replaced by Henry Tudor. It may be thought that people had been too terrified to voice their true feelings while he was alive. But there is no evidence that Richard perpetrated a reign of terror, with government agents infiltrated to keep tabs on sedition, or with suspects disappearing or being questioned under torture as happened in later reigns. If his spies had been that efficient, and his reprisals so terrifying, it's doubtful the rebellion of 1483 would ever have got off the ground.

That Richard's name was blackened by the Tudor regime is an acknowledged fact, although it has been denied that they were responsible for a deliberately crafted campaign of propaganda. This the reader will have to decide, I simply offer what evidence is available.

The earliest surviving record of Tudor denigration of Richard III is Henry Tudor's communication sent from France in 1484, while being financed as a pretender by the French government. Tudor wrote an open letter seeking support for his claim to the English throne, signed 'under our signet' using the royal plural and royal monogram, announcing that the crown of England was rightfully his by 'due and lineal inheritance' (even his greatest admirers never stretched facts that far!). Richard III is described in Tudor's letter as 'that homicide and unnatural tyrant who now unjustly bears dominion over you.' Sentiments like 'homicide and unnatural tyrant' do not occur prior to this.

Tracking the trail of Tudor propaganda, the next example is seen in Wales in 1485. This was where Henry's invading army landed, in the expectation that his Welsh ancestry would win him local recruits, as his French forces marched through Wales on their way to challenge Richard's English defenders. In the process he cultivated the support of the bard Dafydd Llwyd. Upon Henry's victory at Bosworth, Dafydd wrote a poem praising him and condemning Richard with torrents of particularly nasty insults, accusations and personal abuse. Nothing like this exists from any previous date written by any native of Wales, England or even Scotland. There would be a lot more to follow once Tudor was crowned.

Criticism of the last Plantagenet king was of course necessary to justify Henry's takeover process, since he had no 'due and lineal' right to England's throne and no substantive quarrel which warranted killing its occupant.*

Henry had attempted to lead a rebellion against Richard III in 1483, and had been forced to run when it was thoroughly quashed. He ended up in France, where the French, to further their own purposes, decided to support him as a pretender to Richard's throne.

This was fine as long as he was living abroad. But when he returned to England at the head of an army, he needed to justify his invasion to Englishmen. And when he found himself wearing the crown he had to position himself as saving the country from a tyrant. Doubtless with each resistance to Henry's oppressive rule, each uprising and each plot in favour of restoring the previous dynasty, his regime felt rocked to its fragile foundations. And so Richard III's alleged tyranny had to be a Tudor article of faith, and his alleged killing of the princes an essential tool not only to vilify his reputation, but also to indoctrinate the belief that they were actually dead, not merely biding their time to return and threaten Henry's security.

*For anyone interested in Henry VII's ancestry, here it is in summary. His father was the son of an illicit liaison, afterwards identified as a marriage between a Welsh squire and the French widow of Henry V, Katherine de Valois. On his mother's side he was descended from a bastard half-brother of Henry IV, who had been legitimated by Parliament but barred from the crown. Thus he inherited Plantagenet blood from his mother, but from the wrong side of the blanket. At the time he seized the throne, even if one disregards this prohibition, there were at least 16 living (legitimate) Lancastrian heirs ahead of him in the succession, not to mention at least 13 heirs of the house of York.

4
REASONABLE DOUBTS

As we saw from Dafydd Llwyd through to William Shakespeare, the Tudor depiction of Richard III prevailed for over 100 years. There was understandably little desire to argue on the part of ordinary people.

But the dynastic obsessions of the Tudors came to nothing when their line petered out with the virgin queen, Elizabeth I. At this time, around 1600, a scholarly antiquarian movement arose in England. The antiquaries had a new and different approach which valued ascertaining the realities of history as corroborated by proof, and they were responsible for searching out and collecting innumerable old documents and manuscripts (which now form some of the most precious collections in the British Library).

They demanded a high standard of scholarship at their meetings, and if anyone gave a talk or wrote a treatise, they had to back up what they said with evidence. It was probably for lack of evidence that some of them began to question the lurid stories about Richard III, and in particular some, including John Stow, expressed doubt whether he killed the 'Princes in the Tower'.

The first full-scale book in Richard's defence – and it was a very long and detailed one – was written in 1619 by the antiquary Sir George Buck, Master of the Revels at the court of King James I.

Buck had a tremendous interest in genealogy, and took pride that one of his ancestors had been in Richard III's service. He had accessed several important manuscripts dating from Richard's time, and used them to illustrate his case.

One of them was Richard's Act of Succession, known as *Titulus*

Horace Walpole, 4th Earl of Oxford

Regius. This was the Act of Parliament that confirmed Richard III's title to the crown of England, which Henry VII had ordered repealed over a century previously and prevented anyone from reading.

This discovery was a revelation because when the Act had been suppressed by Henry Tudor on seizing the throne, he thought he'd had every copy destroyed so that nobody knew the facts it contained. In ignorance of these facts Thomas More wrote all sorts of erroneous and misleading information in his *History of King Richard III*, which people like Buck were at last able to recognize for the fiction it was.

Buck devoted a great amount of time and energy to his revisionist book, which made some very useful points. But he died soon afterwards and was eventually sidelined by history.

A much bigger splash was made by Horace Walpole in the 18th century with his *Historic Doubts on the Life and Reign of King Richard III* (1768). Horace, son of Sir Robert Walpole, was a prominent antiquary and man of letters who, partly inspired by Buck, came out with all guns blazing in a frontal attack on the nonsenses written by Thomas More, describing him as someone who could use truth 'as a cement in a fabric of fiction'.

Walpole's *Historic Doubts* led the charge in what is now characterized as the Great Debate. As his modern editor comments, it 'lit a crackling fire of controversy'. His book was a best-seller and caused a great stir, and it certainly convinced some 18th-century historians that Richard III was not as described by Tudor tradition. But Walpole's approach was immoderate and his research was scarcely faultless. It was not an assessment of Richard's life and reign, rather it was a polemic which whipped up outraged debate, and the resulting controversy served in some quarters to reinforce the stridency of the traditionalists. So it won few converts to the cause of seriously re-evaluating the reputation of Richard himself.

The first truly scholarly attempt at getting to grips with the historical Richard was the biography published in 1844 by Caroline Halsted, a brilliant and thorough appraisal (and a favourable one) based on exhaustive research. A two-part review in the literary magazine *Athenaeum* applauded the care with which Halsted sought out and marshalled her many authorities, and concluded:

> Although we may not believe Richard to have been quite so blameless as she attempts to prove him, we willingly allow that his real character was widely different from that which tradition and Tudor history have assigned to him.

Halsted's biography, which is still in print, pioneered the basis for an evidence-based analysis, gathering together most of the source material that has been used by historians ever since. The Victorians weighed in throughout the rest of the century with arguments for and against, but at least there were now many more referenced and contextualized facts on which opinions could be formed.

Nevertheless, the great awe in which Shakespeare was by now held, and the even greater reverence attached to the memory of Sir Thomas More (who was set on the path to sainthood in 1886), meant that any who chose to diverge from the traditional view had to do so in small ways and with careful steps. In fact that grand old historian of the Victorian era, James Gairdner, who found many virtues in Richard and his reign ('he seems really to have studied his country's welfare'), came down at the end in favour of the tradition that he was a villain for the very reason, as he explained, that he felt unable to resist the great weight of so many centuries.

* * *

In the last hundred years Richard III has had his supporters and detractors. For readability, the most attractive story of his life was Paul Murray Kendall's *Richard III* of 1955, and from the 'scientific' standpoint the standard biography was that written by Charles Ross in 1981. Both are now well out of date.

Generally speaking it's uncontested that there is no tangible evidence that Richard was guilty of the various crimes (particularly the murders) laid at his door. Nevertheless he was a human being who wielded enormous power, made mistakes, sometimes acted rashly and ill-advisedly, and inevitably made enemies. Whether some of his actions were 'illegal' is a difficult question, and one that arises in relation to any mediaeval king. Even his contemporaries would have been hard put to agree on an answer. So we need to be clear that what we are discussing here is essentially interpretation, whether positive or negative.

Probably the greatest waste of energy on the part of the two sides of the debate has been sniping at each other rather than addressing each other's arguments. One writer expressed the feeling that traditional historians must be some kind of alien beings who had 'drifted here from outer space', while Ricardians have been dubbed 'a quasi-religious cult of adulation' which believes those who disagree with it will 'burn in hell'.

It's understandable that those on the side of Richard tend to lose patience with traditionalists who adopt a general air of superior knowledge while quoting second-hand assumptions and unsupported evidence. 'Prove your case!' is the Ricardian cry, but it is usually up to them to prove theirs. The Ricardian heresy tends to attract people who take pains to delve into the evidence for and against, so they find it tedious having constantly to confront the same arguments. Perhaps even worse is dealing with simplistic terms like 'goodie' or 'baddie', 'hero' or 'villain'.

At the same time it's hard for anyone brought up with the traditional view of Richard, as taught for generations in schools and universities, to set aside what they believe, hear and see reiterated all the time, unless it comes with the full and weighty sanction of authority behind it. After all, UFOlogists also claim to have conducted exhaustive investigations and researches, so why should Ricardians expect a serious hearing for their oddball ideas and conspiracy theories?

There is a wide spectrum of revisionist views ranging from mild to hotly opinionated, so it serves no good purpose to brand them all extremist, any more than for Ricardians to generalize about all who hold to the traditional view. Much more useful is to look at actual records of past events as they happened and were perceived by Richard's contemporaries. And, when a person's interpretation is encountered, to ask yourself 'how did the writer know that?'.

Which means that now, as I prepare to take you back more than 500 years, I should make it clear that I propose to stick to whatever evidence is revealed in the writings that survive from those times.

Elizabeth Woodville, queen to Edward IV

5
DID RICHARD III USURP THE THRONE?

In this little book it is not the intention to tell the full story of King Richard III, who ruled England from June 1483 to August 1485. It is purely an attempt to explain the controversy that surrounds him. The most well known part of that controversy is whether he was responsible for killing the 'Princes in the Tower', who disappeared during his reign in one of the most famous mysteries of English history.

Inextricable from the fate of the princes is their importance in the English royal line of succession, so we need to start with this. The reason being that the succession was changed when they were removed and replaced by Richard. This process has been called usurpation, and the argument is that if he stole the crown from the princes, he must have wanted them dead so that they couldn't take it back. So we'll start with this term 'usurpation', and explore the historical reasons that explain how Richard III came to be king.

King Edward IV dies

The boys known as the 'Princes in the Tower' were the two sons of King Edward IV by Elizabeth (*née* Woodville) who became his queen in 1464.

Edward IV died on 9 April 1483 at the age of nearly 41, leaving seven living children by Elizabeth and a few more by his mistresses. Richard III did not become king immediately. He was Edward's youngest and last surviving brother, so these children were Edward's heirs and Richard's nephews.

Richard was Duke of Gloucester at this time, aged 30 and living with his wife and son in the North of England, where the king depended on him to rule as a viceroy taking care of the turbulent North and border territory. Under Edward's foreign policy England was currently in a state of barely contained war with Scotland, while he had recently started preparing for renewed hostilities against France. For many years Richard had been his brother's leading general, and of late had been taking charge in the absence of the king as commander in battle. To be precise, the offices he held under Edward IV were Great Chamberlain of England, High Constable of England, Lord High Admiral of England, and Lieutenant General of England's land forces.

In the usual tradition, as soon as the late king died his eldest son immediately succeeded. Thus the elder of the princes ceased to be Prince of Wales and became King Edward V in April 1483, aged 12 years and 5 months. His younger brother Richard, Duke of York, was aged 9 years and 8 months. In this book we will continue to call them 'princes' because that is how they have been known for centuries.

As Prince of Wales Edward had been trained for monarchy since the age of three, residing with his own household in Ludlow, but subject to the governorship of a group of nobles, principal among whom were relatives of the queen, led by her senior brother and head of the Woodville family, Anthony, Earl Rivers. The boy's other governors included his half-brother Sir Richard Grey, the younger of Elizabeth's two sons by her previous marriage to Sir John Grey (she was a widow when the king met her). Her elder son, Thomas Grey, Marquess of Dorset, seems to have spent more of his time at court in the company of King Edward IV, where he was identified among the 'promoters and companions of his vices'.

The late king's death at Westminster Palace being sudden and unexpected, Edward V was still far away in Ludlow when it happened. Given that messengers could take several days to make such a journey, and an equal number to return, the new young king could not be expected to have all arrangements in place to arrive in proper style at Westminster with his retinue before the end of April. Richard of Gloucester was also several days' journey away in Yorkshire when he heard the news. In their absence the Council of

Edward V

the late king, consisting of leading lords, magnates, clerics and other hand-picked advisers, held the reins of government.

There was some disquiet and disagreement within the Council as they considered the implications of rule by a child. The chronicle of Crowland Abbey contains a note that some of the more far-sighted members felt that young Edward V should not be left entirely under the control of his mother's family. But it was rather too late to change things at this stage without crossing the Woodvilles whom Edward IV had purposely elevated to considerable power and prestige. In any case, they had representatives who were on the spot at Westminster Palace when he died.

So in Council at Westminster it was the Woodvilles' decisions that prevailed when it came to actions taken immediately after the king's death, including the launching of an expensive seagoing force ordered by two of the queen's relatives, simultaneously draining the treasury and undermining Richard of Gloucester's command of England's forces on land and sea.

A prominent Council member who had reservations about their actions was William, Lord Hastings, one of Edward IV's oldest and closest friends. Hastings was committed to the young prince's succession and had enjoyed an important role in his upbringing, but he had a history of personal feuding with some of the Woodvilles, principally Anthony, Earl Rivers. When it was proposed that Rivers should raise a further substantial armed force, to be brought with him to London as young Edward V's escort, Lord Hastings openly opposed the move. Hastings enjoyed control of a large force of his own, which made his threats perilous to resist, so a compromise was reached limiting the king's escort to a not ungenerous 2,000 men.

Moves to govern England

Normally in England the convention was that until a child-king reached years of discretion, the realm would be ruled in his name by a Lord Protector, a senior adult male of the royal blood. Of course there was no written precedent laying down these rules, and in the past there had been variations on such arrangements. The recent reign of the last child-king, Henry VI, had suffered ruination at the hands of competing factions who battled to assert influence over him, and as a result England had been blighted by the civil hostilities known nowadays as the 'Wars of the Roses'. The battles had ceased only when Edward IV put an end to them.

There was no precedent for a queen consort or her family to perform the roles of regent or protector, but the Woodvilles had seized the initiative. They were arguing for an early coronation, which would be the first decisive step in enabling Edward V to reign immediately in his own right, assisted by a group of 'many persons' in which Richard would be the titular head. Self-evidently the boy's existing family and mentors would predominate in such a forum, a reality underlined by Thomas Grey who declared, on being advised to wait until Richard had been consulted, 'We are so important that even without the king's uncle we can make and enforce these decisions'.

Although Edward IV's will has not survived, it is reported that he made codicils on his deathbed when he realized he was about to leave his realm in the hands of a twelve-year-old. From clues in a number of commentaries it seems apparent that he intended his brother to assume the mantle of Lord Protector until his son came of age, and that this decision was popular: 'The people ... favoured [Richard] in their hearts from a belief in his probity,' and it was 'commonly said by all' that he 'deserved the government'.

The above statements describing how Richard enjoyed widespread support from the people appeared in a report by the foreign agent Dominic Mancini, writing to his French patron. As already mentioned, this is one of only two surviving narratives of any length which we know were written around the time of the events they describe, in this case 1483. Both, for different reasons, were heavily biased against Richard III. Even so, Mancini set down the following observations about Richard as Duke of Gloucester:

> The good reputation of his private life and public activities powerfully attracted the esteem of strangers. Such was his renown in warfare that whenever a difficult and dangerous policy had to be undertaken, it would be entrusted to his discretion and his generalship.

Richard was thus widely admired for fulfilling the feudal/chivalric role in which fate had cast him, and from which (unlike his late brother the Duke of Clarence) he had never wavered. He fully expected to take action as provided by Edward IV's will and in line with normal precedent.

Unfortunately, with the headstrong actions of the Woodvilles, the scene had been set for conflict even before he arrived at the seat of government. England's enemies would already be looking to exploit any weakness during the minority, so if there were now two factions with opposing intentions as to how England should be ruled, the situation could be very dangerous for the country.

From the way Lord Hastings handled the Woodville plan to raise an army, it will be seen that force of arms often carried the argument at this time. Noble lords and rich magnates were in the habit of gathering together armed retainers to impose their will, whether legal or not, something which can be seen to great effect in the misfortunes of the Paston family in their famous letters. Richard's choice was clear: either to quickly establish that his authority prevailed, or find a *fait accompli* waiting for him on arrival. He made a pre-emptive strike.

Being a seasoned military commander he knew the effectiveness of acting first before your opponent attacks you, so this was how he neutralized the Woodvilles' bid for power, a bid which depended on having the king under their control. Richard arranged a rendezvous with the king's retinue on its way to London at which he simply took command of young Edward V and his escort. He arrested some of the king's leading governors – Earl Rivers, Sir Richard Grey and Sir Thomas Vaughan – and sent them to be held in the North, claiming they had arranged an ambush for him on the road. They were held for several weeks, probably with a view to exerting pressure on the remaining Woodvilles come to terms, but this didn't happen and eventually they were tried and executed.

After five centuries we can ascertain little about the reality of any ambush; although from reports of how the king's route was oddly rearranged at the last minute, so that Richard's party would have to pass through Woodville home territory, it cannot be ruled out. And while Richard's arrests were carried out precipitately and ruthlessly, they were within the executive powers encompassed by his various offices.

One in particular was the office of High Constable of England, conferred on him for life, under which he was authorized to take action in the name of the crown in the event of treason, insurrection or general disorder, or when the king was incapacitated or an interregnum existed. He was empowered summarily to detain, arrest and try in his own court under the Law of Arms, and pronounce sentence without appeal. They were terrible powers, but necessary in the context of an England where the rule of the sword was never far from the surface.

Succession and protectorship

England has never had a written constitution, and still less were the rules of succession to the throne laid down in the Middle Ages. Many kings of England had come to the throne other than as the previous king's son – far more in England than was the case, for example, in the French succession.

Being a member of the ruling royal family was an important qualification, and everything was straightforward when the succession mirrored the ordinary civil norms of property inheritance. But the task of ruling a country was not merely ceremonial: it was a massive job of work, embodying a host of civil and military roles including head of state, prime minister, head of defence and foreign affairs, personal leader of armed forces, head of justice, home secretary and controller of the exchequer.

Monarchy in England also required a degree of assent from those ruled. Thus a capable adult warrior, like Henry IV in 1399, could successfully depose a failing king and set aside a child-heir when he had the necessary support and they had none.

Throughout history deals have been done to determine who should rule England, and in 1460, only 23 years prior to 1483, the succession was removed by Parliament from the then-current heir of Lancaster and conferred on the new ruling house of York. In more recent times we can point to well-known occasions when the heir or incumbent has been replaced at the insistence of the people, the latest being in 1936. So when 'the crime of usurpation' is alleged, it is actually a value-judgement based on the particular scheme of things which *the person alleging the crime* considers to have been improperly overturned. Usurpation, in other words, is in the eyes of the beholder.

Henry IV and his son, Henry V of Agincourt fame, both Plantagenets, established an effective dynasty that descended from the royal house of Lancaster. Unfortunately the trend of success ceased with Henry VI, who came to the throne as an infant and was

45

The child-king Henry VI

mentally unsuited to be king. To make matters worse, he also suffered bouts of losing his reason.

During his reign the country was bankrupted and most of her overseas possessions were lost, while at home he failed to control ambitious magnates who were ruthless in their determination to gain profit and power Those who were excluded coalesced around the royal house of York, and tensions intermittently erupted into battles between the opposing factions (the so-called 'Wars of the Roses'). This series of battles has also been called rather more accurately the 'Cousins Wars' – those cousins being various members of the extended royal family and their respective supporters. The house of York family tree is shown on page 12, and Lancaster on page 48.

The Duke of York was the senior adult of the royal blood during this period, whose sons would later become Edward IV and Richard III. York had been called upon to provide a safe pair of hands as Lord Protector during Henry's spells of incapacity, and had restored a certain amount of order. But as soon as he lost that status he was once more marginalized and excluded from the circles of power, to the point where his position became intolerable.

Although the individual battles in these wars were localized, many thousands of ordinary people and their communities, as well as the overall economy of the country, were forced to suffer the consequences of unrest, death and destruction.

Attempting to resolve the matter constitutionally, York put forward a claim that the throne was rightfully his by succession, not Henry's. Eventually a settlement was reached with Parliament under which the house of York would succeed after Henry VI's death, instead of Henry's own son, Edward of Lancaster. No one would have dreamed of such a thing if the realm had not been sliding into chaos; even Henry VI acceded to the arrangement. But the Lancastrian side rallied to Henry's militant queen who preferred to settle the matter by the sword. As fate would have it they were the eventual losers, whereupon York's son took the throne to popular acclaim as Edward IV in 1461.

During this period the phrase 'usurped the throne' was bandied about quite a lot, each side using it to define the other side's actions. Nor did Edward hold on securely to the crown. Within ten years he had been deposed and Henry VI reinstated; followed quickly by Henry's deposition and Edward's reinstatement again. All of which was still vividly remembered in 1483, especially by those who now faced the prospect of the throne being occupied by another child. And already there were tussles for control of him.

Nothing in life is wholly black or wholly white, and Edward IV had certainly given the queen's Woodville family every reason to believe that he had singled them out for pre-eminence.

But the fact remained that they had been supporters of the Lancastrian party, and the advancement of their numerous family members had closed off opportunities for many noble families who had more illustrious pedigrees, and who had endured much suffering in their long devotion to the house of York.

So the Woodvilles were no strangers to friction and resentment, although (despite Shakespeare's imaginings) there is no record there was any bad feeling with Richard of Gloucester. Nevertheless, when they heard the news that he had taken control of the young king, the queen's family in London attempted to raise an armed force against him. In this attempt they were unsuccessful.

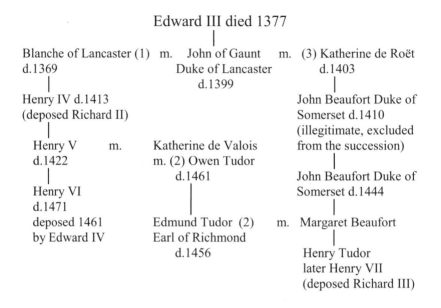

Edward III died 1377

Blanche of Lancaster (1) m. John of Gaunt m. (3) Katherine de Roët
d.1369   Duke of Lancaster   d.1403
                                  d.1399
Henry IV d.1413   John Beaufort Duke of
(deposed Richard II)   Somerset d.1410
                                                   (illegitimate, excluded
   Henry V   m.   Katherine de Valois   from the succession)
   d.1422   m. (2) Owen Tudor
                           d.1461   John Beaufort Duke of
   Henry VI   Somerset d.1444
   d.1471
   deposed 1461   Edmund Tudor (2)   m. Margaret Beaufort
   by Edward IV   Earl of Richmond
                       d.1456   Henry Tudor
                                                   later Henry VII
                                                   (deposed Richard III)

House of Lancaster family tree (simplified)

Their reaction, rather than reconcile and make the best of it, was to hasten into sanctuary at Westminster Abbey.

In case the concept of sanctuary should need explaining, it was often possible in the Middle Ages for fugitives to avoid arrest by claiming refuge at the altar of a church, and some religious houses had special powers to grant long-term sanctuary. Most monasteries also offered accommodation for guests of high and low rank, so at Westminster the queen and her family were housed in the abbot's lodgings. For them to take sanctuary in this way essentially amounted to passive resistance. Despite attempts at negotiation by the King's Council, this remained an unresolved embarrassment.

It may equally well be remarked that, rather than submit to Woodville dominance, Richard Duke of Gloucester had himself chosen a course of confrontation. He would have justified this with the simple fact that rank reigned supreme in the 15th century, and the pre-eminence of the high nobility and blood royal outranked everything else. In Richard's view, by virtue of his royal lineage, his autocratic status in Edward IV's reign, and his several offices in command of England's military might, he did not expect to bend the knee to any man save the king himself.

Although accompanied from York by an entourage of only around 500 retainers, the dominance of his position had been quickly recognized by Edward V's armed escort of 2,000 men who offered no resistance. On his arrival in the capital the Council duly confirmed him in office as Lord Protector, and he assumed power as *de facto* ruler of England during Edward V's minority.

Revelations and repercussions

Having dealt with this lengthy scene-setting, we can now move on to how Richard of Gloucester became Richard III, and the mystery of what became of Edward V and his brother.

Throughout the month of May 1483, Richard as protector presided over royal business while preparations went ahead for Edward V's coronation on 22 June (minting coins, ordering coronation robes, calling Parliament, etc.). The Chancellor was preparing a speech to Parliament stating the endorsement of the Council that Richard's protectorship should continue after the coronation.

In anticipation of all this the new king was now resident in the Royal Apartments at the Tower of London. Far from being the place of dread incarceration it later became under the Tudors, the Tower was at this time London's foremost royal palace from which it was traditional for the king to process formally, in the view of all his people, to be crowned at Westminster Abbey. He was certainly not imprisoned, in evidence of which his mother was persuaded by the Archbishop of Canterbury, a few weeks later, to send his younger brother out of sanctuary to join him.

Then something startling happened at around the end of May which brought about a sudden end to preparations.

This event was best described in the memoirs of Philippe de Commynes, a high-ranking diplomat of the French court and aide to Louis XI in the 1470s–80s, whose business was to know what went on at the royal courts of Europe. Although he wrote his memoirs in the 1490s – a little later than the period of Richard's lifetime – he had not been inculcated with propaganda or silenced by suppression of the facts as happened in Tudor England at that time.

Commynes wrote that the Bishop of Bath and Wells (Robert Stillington) brought Richard of Gloucester the news that he had witnessed an early secret marriage between Edward IV and Eleanor Talbot, a daughter of the Earl of Shrewsbury. She had since died, but had been living when the king married Elizabeth Woodville, which meant that he had committed bigamy. Edward evidently had a fondness for secret liaisons, as his marriage to Elizabeth was also secret, although he admitted to it some months afterwards and had her crowned queen.

Unfortunately, under the complex laws of the Catholic Church, Edward's secret marital shenanigans rendered his offspring, including Edward V, illegitimate. There was no way of mending the situation, nor was the luxury of time available. Edward IV had died leaving England in bellicose relationships with two adjacent powers, in a Europe where acquisitive ruling houses were jostling for power and precedence. It was in this dangerous climate that the King's Council and leading nobility, who were preparing for Edward V's coronation and Parliament, considered the disturbing implications.

There would be many who totally failed to comprehend the contorted laws which made Edward IV's heirs illegitimate and which afforded them no route back to legitimacy (many modern day commentators have the same problem – it takes considerable expertise to understand mediaeval canon law). Others with a stake in the boy king's future would feel he should be crowned in spite of this impediment. Their stance was entirely understandable, especially from the perspective of those whose loyalties and careers were tied into the continuance of the existing court party, where the Woodville family wielded their influence:

> … [the queen] attracted to her party many strangers and introduced them to court, so that they alone should manage the private and public businesses of the crown, surround the king, and have bands of retainers, give or sell offices, and finally rule the very king himself.

This statement was made by the previously mentioned Italian Dominic Mancini after his visit to England in 1483, in a report to his patron Angelo Cato, a leading adviser to the French king – Mancini had been asked by Cato to provide intelligence for use by the French court. Apparently Mancini spoke very little English, and as he was writing for an anti-English audience he undoubtedly depicted England's rulers in a deliberately negative light; but on the other hand the theme of his report was to convey the scandal of how the throne was seized by Richard III, so it served little purpose to paint an excessively distorted picture of the Woodvilles. As with many comments we will encounter on our way in this story, it may need to be taken with a pinch of salt. But the essential fact remains that the Woodville party had been dominant at court since the mid 1460s.

With two of their party at large and organizing counter-moves, and with those in sanctuary refusing to emerge and acknowledge Richard's protectorship, the Woodvilles provided a logical nexus for resistance. Letters have survived from Richard to his supporters in the North dated 10–11 June urgently calling for troops to be mustered to come to his aid in response to plots against him by 'the queen, her blood adherents and affinity'.

Apparently more details soon became known to him, as his calls to arms were quickly followed by a shocking incident on 13 June when he arrested a group of plotters led by the popular and powerful

Lord Hastings, whom he accused of entering his presence with hidden weapons to launch a surprise attack on him. Although Mancini reported this as a 'false pretext of treason', it would have been a capital offence against the office of the Lord Protector.

Hastings was executed that same day, while five or six others suspected of involvement in the conspiracy were arrested (they all survived, and most were freed quite soon afterwards). Aspects of Hastings's swift conviction and condemnation suggest that he was sentenced under the Law of Arms which dealt explicitly with treason and insurrection, with Richard acting in his office as High Constable of England.

Readers must decide for themselves whether this accusation was a pretence, as characterized by Richard's detractors who identified it as his first move on the slippery slope towards seizing the throne. Or was Hastings leading a real and dangerous conspiracy which earned for him the inevitable bloody retribution of those violent times?

Many commentators adopt the line that Hastings was an innocent victim who had to be removed because he stood between Richard and the crown. This derives from the assumption that Richard's underlying intention all along was to seize power, which conforms to the opinions of the two main narrators of the day, Dominic Mancini and the Crowland author, despite documentary evidence that shows his own plan was to crown Edward V and continue as protector. The aforementioned assumption gets even more complicated at this point, because it must further assume, without proof, that he falsely manufactured the story of Edward IV's bigamy. Otherwise, if his nephews actually were illegitimate, then it would be right for Richard to succeed his brother and Hastings was wrong to oppose him (which he clearly did, or he would not have been executed).

Whichever way you look at it, Hastings cannot be characterized as an innocent victim, especially at a time when no decision had yet been made about changing the succession in Richard's favour. Hastings was, in fact, a politically savvy player throughout Edward IV's reign and was no stranger to coercion (remember that he used threats the previous month to prevent the Woodvilles from descending on the capital with a large army).

Mancini comments, additionally, that three of those arrested – Lord Hastings, Bishop Morton and Archbishop Rotherham – were known to have 'foregathered in each other's houses', which sounds more like a conspiracy than a charge dreamed up against Hastings out of the blue. And, of course, we have seen that Richard already had suspicions which led him to call for northern reinforcements.

As in so many cases with Richard III, we are here confronted with a situation capable of different interpretations: either we agree with Hastings's group who assumed he was aiming for the crown and had to be removed; or we accept that Richard's actions arose from a disinclination to be assassinated.

A recurring problem is that we have only two coherent narratives from Richard's day – Mancini and Crowland – which purport to set out what happened, but instead of recounting facts straightforwardly they both intrude their own spin on events, presuming to know all about the underhand thought-processes that motivated Richard's actions (one of them even relates his dreams!).

Since no positive account has survived from the pen of a supporter, it is risky to rely on hostile narratives for the unvarnished truth. But even though we haven't yet discovered a chronicle written by, say, one of Richard's northern partisans, nevertheless there are brief references to be found in other sources which offer no editorializing about 'false pretexts'.

One particular scribbled note expresses extreme concern for the fate of several named individuals, including Richard himself. Another, written by an unknown citizen of London, simply refers matter-of-factly to some persons having been discovered plotting his death, and states that Hastings paid the price with his head.

A clearer view is gained if the incident is seen, as these people saw it, in the light of events of the day, rather than in the light of hindsight.

The deposition of Edward V

Meanwhile the news of Edward IV's two marriages and their effect on the succession was doubtless being heatedly discussed and investigated. Modern experts on canon law have written lengthy explanations of how Edward painted himself into a corner from which there was no retrieving the situation, the greatest difficulty being that both his marriages were carried out in secret in defiance of

Church law. Having dug that kind of a hole for yourself, there just wasn't a way of climbing back out (especially if you were dead).

This was a succession crisis of major proportions, and England could not afford to waste time while her enemies were making ready to take advantage of any interregnum or lapse of command at the helm. The prospect of a child on the throne already rendered the country vulnerable, and even more so with opposing parties vying to control him. Once that child's very legitimacy had come into question, the door was open not only to foreign aggression, but to any opportunistic strong-arm faction that might try to revive a new-style 'Cousins War' all over again. This is, in fact, precisely what happened a few months later, but support for it was fragmentary and the attempted rebellion was put down.

The King's Council took the decision to postpone Edward V's coronation to a date in November, but apparently the planned sitting of Parliament in June was not cancelled. A couple of writs of cancellation were sent out, but from the fact that London was soon thronged with the arrival of parliamentary representatives and their retinues, clearly the despatch of cancellations was ceased as soon as it began. It seems likely that Richard desired to follow the precedent set by his father, who had looked to Parliament to take the role of adjudicator in such matters.

Although Parliament was not opened by Edward V and therefore did not sit officially, the lords and magnates of the realm were reported as assembling to consider the matter in consultation with the leading civic dignitaries of London. They took the pragmatic decision that they could not accept the risks of a reign (and dynasty) that carried the taint of bastardy. Setting aside the offspring of Edward IV, they composed a petition to Richard in which he was asked to become king. He accepted, and his reign began on 26 June.

This, then, is how Richard III came to the throne, a process which his opponents saw as usurpation. In the new year he would call his own sitting of Parliament at which an Act of Succession was adopted, known afterwards as *Titulus Regius*.

It reiterated the text of the petition from the parliamentary representatives in June 1483, giving the full details of how Edward IV had already entered into a secret contract of marriage with Lady Eleanor, daughter of the Earl of Shrewsbury, when he subsequently entered into another secret marriage with Elizabeth Woodville – and in consequence 'all th'Issue and Children of the seid King Edward been Bastards, and unable to inherite or to clayme any thing by Inheritance, by the Law and Custome of Englond'. Thus Richard was called upon to take the throne 'accordyng to this Eleccion of us the Thre Estates of this Lande, as by youre true Enherritaunce'.

As if to underline the unanimity of the leading magnates, Richard's coronation on 6 July was attended by almost the entire peerage of England, both Yorkist and Lancastrian.

The anti-Richard argument

The argument that Richard was viewed in his own day as seizing the crown illegally derives from the opinions recorded in hostile narratives. The intelligence-gatherer Mancini has been mentioned already, and naturally he played to the anti-English prejudices of his French masters. One would scarcely expect him to hand in a report that applauded the wise and thoughtful decisions made by the English Parliament!

We also have that other substantial narrative source for this period which is the chronicle of Crowland Abbey, an account of domestic activities at the abbey combined with an anonymous parallel account of events in the world of politics and government, compiled and written into a continuous narrative by the monks.

The section about Richard III's reign displays an undisguised bias against him and the whole North of England where his support was concentrated. It was long thought to have been the work of his Lord Chancellor, Bishop John Russell, reinforcing the traditional perception that Richard came to be universally denigrated, even by his own chancellor. The idea of Russell as author has lost favour with modern scholars, who have now suggested a variety of quite low-ranking chancery officials as possibly responsible. However, because of its supposed composition by such a leading character, historians assumed for a very long time that it was a reflection of the general feeling of the day, a misconception found widely in books and articles which will not be dispelled any time soon.

The anti-Richard position taken by the chronicle, and by those believing in its authority, is that the revelation of Edward IV's secret bigamous marriages came far too conveniently, and must have been manufactured so that Richard could depose his brother's children.

With the scarcity of documentary evidence presently available, this is an argument incapable of proof either way. Secret marriages self-evidently leave no paper trail, and disbelief in secret marriages is patently a matter of opinion. Neither Stillington nor Richard committed his innermost thoughts and schemes to paper, so there is nothing to tell us whether the story was genuine or cooked up.

To test the 'too convenient to be true' argument we should perhaps look at how it was viewed in June 1483 by the leading representatives of Parliament. They had the hard choice to make, and they had Bishop Stillington there in person to quiz and probe. They must have made enquiries and sought other witnesses, whether for or against. Indeed many of them would have had long-standing relationships with the queen and her Woodville family, and must have tried to extract information from them.

We have references in various writings confirming the secret nature of Edward IV's Woodville marriage, and there are reports – even public charges – that he was bewitched into it. That much is on record. But although there is evidence that Edward had dealings and personal interactions with Eleanor Talbot and her family, there is nothing reliable to confirm his secret marriage to her. At the time it was not required, or even customary, to make written records of marriages. Yet neither is there anything in any record of the time *refuting* the story, or even reporting that anyone *tried* to refute it. And as history shows, Richard was offered the throne on the strength of it.

The Crowland chronicle gives the full story of the prior marriage which is described as 'the pretext' for the deposition of Edward V, which is how you would have looked at it if you objected to the outcome, and indeed the anonymous author was clearly scandalized. But despite being so vehemently negative about Richard, he doesn't actually say that it was mistaken, or implausible, or a tissue of lies. He is more concerned that it hasn't been submitted to the proper ecclesiastical court for adjudication. He faithfully records the terms of the petition, and all the details he gives can be corroborated with those in the later Act of Parliament, *Titulus Regius*.

A possible litmus test of the story's credibility resides in how Henry VII dealt with it when he took the throne after Richard's death. His justices recommended subjecting it – and Stillington as its instigator – to a full public investigation, but instead he hushed it all up, and having thoroughly hounded, terrified and imprisoned the hapless bishop he quietly issued him with a pardon.

When Richard III came to the throne in June 1483 on the strength of Stillington's testimony there was, naturally, mistrust and incomprehension on many levels. An abiding opposition to the house of York, and hence to Richard, was already ingrained in those surviving Lancastrians who considered them a dynasty of bloodstained usurpers, a view also echoed by some present-day commentators.

Another substantial faction supported Edward V in spite of everything and objected to Richard supplanting him. At the head of this faction was the Woodville family and their adherents, who foresaw an end to their hopes of being the ruling power. Their leaders were soon whipping up resistance.

It goes without saying that once the tussle for power had been initiated, there had to be a winning party and a losing party. People in mediaeval times knew very well the potential price for challenging the king – they knew the risks and were prepared to take the gamble, so it was not a case of blundering into a situation with their eyes closed.

They could have made their peace and accepted the position which clearly had the backing of the members of Parliament gathered in London, a body which at this time was gradually growing in status and influence. But instead they fomented armed rebellion with the aim of eliminating Richard and restoring Edward V.

In the process, they deliberately revived the old faction-fighting which had blighted England during Henry VI's reign, re-igniting the feud between Lancaster and the ruling Yorkists. They did this by spreading their tentacles to the Continent, allying themselves with a prominent Lancastrian, Henry Tudor, who was living in self-imposed exile in Brittany having refused to reconcile with the house of York. Though they supposed they had enlisted him to the cause of Edward V, the truth of the matter was that Tudor and his ambitious family and supporters were all the while looking to further their own interests.

One may sympathize with the losing side, and one can certainly sympathize with the little boy who was deprived of the crown. Nor can it be claimed that Richard's accession to the throne was bloodless, although the number of deaths involved may be counted on the fingers of one hand. But the actions of his opponents, and the bloodshed and civil strife to which they subjected the people of England in furthering their objectives, are difficult to justify.

6
THE 'PRINCES IN THE TOWER'

Let us examine what we know of the events surrounding the mysterious disappearance of the princes.

While the representatives of England's lords and commons were agonizing over the succession, Edward V and his younger brother, Richard of York, remained in their palace apartments at the Tower with their retinue of servants and clerics, free to play and practise archery in the gardens, and presumably also pursuing their lessons.

The Italian cleric Dominic Mancini, whom we met earlier, made a useful contact in the person of Edward V's physician, John Argentine, who is assumed to have been the main source of Mancini's information about the boy king. Although no physical ailment was mentioned, Dr Argentine made much of his charge's understandably dejected state of mind:

> … the young king, like a victim prepared for sacrifice, sought remission of his sins by daily confession and penance, because he believed death was facing him.

Mancini is one reporter we can be sure was in or around London during the period he described, i.e. the first half of 1483. Even after he left he was evidently seeking information about what happened to Edward V and his brother, right up till December. The overall theme of Mancini's account was Richard's insatiable lust for the crown of England, yet he was unable in all conscience to report that the boys were killed. A careful translation from Mancini's Latin yields the information that 'after Edward IV's children had been set aside, Richard claimed the throne for himself'. The Italian did, however, note that Edward V's original attendants were changed pursuant to discovery of the Hastings plot, after which he and his brother were:

> withdrawn into the inner apartments of the Tower proper, and day by day began to be seen more rarely behind the bars and windows, till at length they ceased to appear altogether.

These were clearly intended to be ominous words. However, Mancini's account consisted mainly of second-hand information, and he pretended no personal access to the protector, the court, the council or the palace. Employing all his skills as a narrator, his best first-hand observation about Edward V was couched as a doom-laden prognosis:

> I have seen many men burst forth into tears and lamentations when mention was made of Edward V after he had been removed from sight; and already there was a suspicion that he had been taken away by death.

If he truly had met these tearful persons (were they Londoners?) it must have been before early July of 1483 when he apparently left England. We have other reasonably reliable information (see below) which leads us to deduce that Edward was still residing in the Tower with his brother throughout July and August, so it is hard to know what value to place on Mancini's augury of doom. As befitted an honest and faithful agent, having established the requisite aura of foreboding, he then went on to confirm that he had made diligent enquiries to discover the truth of the matter … but at the date of making his record (December 1483) had learned precisely nothing:

> Whether, however, he has been taken by death, and by what manner of death, so far I have not at all discovered.

There is no other reliable account written in Richard's reign that ventures an opinion as to what became of the boys (the description 'reliable' is used in the sense that the informant is known to have been in or near London at the time and/or in a position to ferret out facts).

What do we really know for sure?

Since the accusation that Richard III killed his nephews is the foremost allegation against him, we must scrupulously consider all the relevant evidence. After this we must spend some time examining the implications of what we have learned. Fortunately, because this small book is designed to shine an intense spotlight on this subject, there will be space to go into some detail as we progress.

The biggest recurring problem is the wealth of unreliable Tudor-era accounts after Richard's death together with a scarcity of written sources during his lifetime. The only substantial narrative that we know for sure was written entirely during Richard's reign is the previously quoted report of the overtly prejudiced Mancini, whose lack of English meant he had to rely on what he was told.

The other roughly contemporaneous account, which we have also met already, is the relevant section of the chronicle of Crowland Abbey. But there is doubt about the exact date it was written by the monks (probably it was completed after October 1485), and no one knows who the author was. Presumably he was an English cleric, and apparently he had connections with chancery and the King's Council, although his access to the inner circles of government seemed to diminish under the Ricardian regime. He clearly favoured the Woodville cause and had nothing good to say of Richard III, unlike Mancini, who reported the respect that existed for his public and private reputation.

Both writers were keen to record Richard's supposed thoughts and motivations together with their personal interpretations of them.

These are the sum total of *narratives* dating from the 1480s telling the story of Richard's actions, and although they cannot be discounted, they must both be recognized as deliberately taking a negative view. From other sources we pick up a few unguarded comments scattered around in letters and papers, and these can provide some of the most useful clues since they were not written as a exercise in setting out a particular argument.

It is already clear that the Great Debate arose in later years because some people found it difficult if not impossible to believe what was written about Richard III during the reigns of the Tudors after his death; this is why we are concentrating on what can be culled from sources much closer in time to the events they were describing.

Yet the fact that something was recorded during Richard's reign or soon afterwards doesn't necessarily mean that it is truthful or accurate. People then were considerably less well informed about public affairs than nowadays, and lines of communication depended on information passed from person to person, with what degree of veracity is open to question.

They were more credulous, more superstitious, and were taught that God actively punished evil deeds. The devout were expected to draw moral conclusions from the downfall of men. So, since Richard was eventually defeated in battle, even if they could not identify specific actions as intrinsically evil, they often wrote with confidence of foul intentions underlying fair deeds.

Mentioning these caveats will explain why so much attention in these pages is paid not just to what was reported, but by whom, when and where, and whether they had an agenda we can know or make an educated guess at.

What the sources say

It is known that on the advice of the Duke of Buckingham, newly installed as Richard's right-hand man, the princes were lodged at the Tower of London where they enjoyed free roam while they awaited Edward V's coronation.

Over the centuries various kings had moved the Royal Apartments to different areas of the palace to suit their requirements, and by 1483 they were sited in the recently refurbished Lanthorn Tower which had an adjacent garden where the boys were seen playing. The later tradition that they were kept in the 'Bloody Tower' is a myth that the 21st-century Tower of London authorities choose to perpetuate, for reasons best known to themselves.

Nothing amiss is reported until after the Hastings affair, when Mancini speaks of their servants being replaced:

> But after Hastings was removed, all the attendants who had waited upon the king were debarred access to him. He and his brother were withdrawn into the inner apartments of the Tower proper, and day

by day began to be seen more rarely [etc] ... The physician Argentine [was] the last of his attendants whose services the king enjoyed.

With revolt detected even at the heart of the governing council, it would be a relevant precaution to replace Edward V's former attendants with new ones who had been carefully vetted. Among the scanty records for the period we can identify wages paid to fourteen named servants of his in the third week of July, so it would be wrong to suppose that Mancini's description meant a total ban on royal attendants.

Of course it was very sad that the brothers Edward and Richard had to suffer the loss of their accustomed royal retinue, and even more sad that their liberty had to be curtailed through the actions of Hastings and his fellow-conspirators. What was saddest of all was that their father's irresponsible behaviour with women had left them in a sort of limbo where everything they had expected from life was thrown into doubt, leaving their fate in the hands of men whose primary concern was not the boys' personal expectations but the question of who controlled the kingdom. On the other hand, as royal princes they knew it was not unusual for the mettle of kings to be tested by the unpredictabilities of fortune.

Their position was made even more precarious by the next event we hear about, which was a foiled plot to abduct them while Richard III, who had departed on 19 July, was away on progress around England. The rather optimistic scheme involved a group of men who planned to start diversionary fires in various parts of London while the brothers were 'stolen out of the Tower'. One of the plotters was a wardrober who actually worked at the Tower, so it is fair to assume he knew that the brothers were still alive and in residence at the time. The date of this is not known for sure, but a letter written by Richard III from Oxfordshire at the end of July may well refer to it.

Another arrest for plotting at the beginning of August, involving the half-brother of Lady Margaret Beaufort (of whom more later), suggests further actions in pursuit of removing Richard III and restoring Edward V. And meanwhile Richard continued on his progress through Worcestershire, Warwickshire and Leicestershire. He arrived at York at the beginning of September, where he held a solemn investiture of his only son, Edward, aged about seven, as Prince of Wales.

September 1483

The chronicle of Crowland Abbey provides a fairly detailed description of the events of the summer of 1483. The author was among those people who objected to the basis on which Richard III took the throne, and described it as 'sedition and infamy'. He also criticized Richard for wasting money, condemning this in a lengthy passage which described the lavish investiture ceremonies at York for the Prince of Wales. After this the author resumed reporting events on home turf in the south of England:

> In the meantime and while these things were happening the two sons of King Edward remained in the Tower of London with a specially appointed guard.

The celebrations in York culminated on 8 September, so this appears to indicate that up to about this date Edward and his brother Richard were still residing in the Tower. Polydore Vergil's account also agrees with this date. Within the same section of the Crowland narrative it is reported that people in certain areas of the south and west were forming groups with the aim of removing them. More than this, a rumour is mentioned (just one of several rumours garnered by this busy chronicler) that plans were afoot to spirit their sisters away overseas in disguise, 'in case any human fate inside the Tower were to befall the male children'. So far, then, despite rumoured forebodings, at least this particular chronicler considered the boys to be as yet unharmed.

The Crowland author then continues providing quite a full catalogue of information about the progress of the short-lived rebellion that was raised in the summer/autumn of 1483 to restore Edward V. In fact, from some of the details mentioned, there are hints that he had access to its thinking and planning.

After revealing how the Duke of Buckingham surprised everyone by turning against Richard and proclaiming himself rebel leader (which must have been in September), the chronicle goes on to

64

relate: 'a rumour arose that King Edward's sons, by some unknown manner of violent destruction, had met their fate'.

This rumour served to convince the rebels that it would be 'all over with them' unless they found someone to replace Buckingham who, despite his ambitions (perhaps aimed at the crown itself) seemed unable to inspire their loyalty. In his stead they turned to Henry Tudor – son of Lady Margaret Beaufort, Countess of Richmond – who was living with his uncle in Brittany. Both were Lancastrian partisans who had fled England when the forces of Lancaster were defeated by Edward IV.

In view of the uniqueness of the Crowland chronicle, it is important to evaluate the information it contains relating to the disappearance of Edward IV's sons, and to note that nowhere does it say that anyone killed them.

Bearing in mind that a lot of it is prejudiced, gossipy, even purely speculative, there would have been nothing to deter this chronicle from saying that Richard put the boys to death. Or that people believed he did. For by the time the overall account in the chronicle concluded in 1486, Richard III was dead, his reputation was in shreds, and Henry Tudor was on the throne, with no shortage of writers vying to curry favour by denigrating the late king. As the historian Michael Hicks has observed, the chronicle's anti-Ricardian and pro-Tudor stance 'indicates how very early and effective was the promulgation of the Tudor myth'.

Yet the Crowland chronicle never intimated, whether as fact or opinion, that Edward IV's sons had died, still less been put to death. Although vehemently disapproving of Richard's actions upon seizing the throne from his nephews, the writer seemed principally concerned at the process employed to deprive them of their inheritance. Their 'cause' is said to have been avenged at Bosworth.

Despite the chronicle's many failings, the portion that deals with the rebellion is very accurate where it can be checked with official records. It demonstrates a familiarity with the twists and turns of events as they progressed which makes it a very credible narrative. It is, in fact, the only surviving account written close to when the rebellion was taking place, by someone who was sufficiently interested to record the kinds of details an informed commentator might obtain.

Henry Tudor, the victor at the battle of Bosworth,
later Henry VII

In particular the chronology of this section is quite impressive. As confirmed by independent sources, it is correct in summarizing that opposition to Richard on Edward V's behalf had been simmering right up through late July and early August, remaining low-key until Buckingham became involved in September.

Things were much more active across the Channel, where the Tudor camp in Brittany had been augmented by the arrival of the queen's brother, Sir Edward Woodville, with ships and treasure to further the objective of restoring his sister's son to the throne. A Woodville-Tudor alliance was soon formed, and by late August the Duke of Brittany had been prevailed upon to assist their proposed invasion of England in support of Edward V's restoration.

The rumour that changed all their plans (which is crucial to the allegation that the boys were killed), could scarcely have been spread before the middle of September. On 16 September Richard III was still authorizing payments to be made to Buckingham, so at this date he was not even aware that the duke had proclaimed the rebellion and his leadership of it. It was soon after this proclamation that the rumour is said to have arisen, which led the rebels to drop Buckingham in favour of Henry Tudor as their leader. Though Crowland doesn't mention it, Tudor's Breton-equipped fleet helps to explain why this unlikely champion presented such an attractive alternative for the English rebels.

To conclude the story of the rebellion, which eventually struck in October 1483, it was quickly put down by forces loyal to Richard III. Adverse weather delayed Henry Tudor's crossing of the Channel, and his ships were forced to turn back when they found the wrong kind of welcome awaiting them. The same weather also prevented the Duke of Buckingham's attempts to lead his reluctant forces out from Wales, and eventually he was handed over to face justice. He was executed on 2 November.

The rumour – why believe it?

The Crowland chronicle may sometimes stretch credulity too far, but at least in this instance the writer is scrupulous not to call a rumour a fact.

If this rumour – spread amid the frenzied climate of a rebellion – seems a rather thin basis from which to construe a double murder, we must remember that the conclusions of many centuries are very much influenced by the 'Tudor myth' incorporating James Tyrell's supposed confession as recounted by Thomas More.

For historians in former ages the existence of such pre-digested information was a godsend, especially when it was reported by what seemed to be authoritative writers. Although today the idea of totally setting aside this uncorroborated confession story still seems a step too far, hopefully we may be permitted to request a modicum of proof before it is accepted as conclusive evidence.

Truth, they say, is the first casualty of war, and the Tudors were not alone in blackening the names of those they needed to destroy. The cynical politics of the Tudor age and Henry VII's personal disregard for truth are well known and documented, e.g. his pretence of a rightful claim to the crown of England by 'due and lineal inheritance'. So with all this Tudor spin flying about, it is wise to be wary about taking anything on trust.

On the other hand, there would be no Great Debate if it were not possible that the rumour could actually have been true. This is why the evidence in its favour, scanty though it is, must be carefully weighed.

Most serious historians who believe the princes were killed argue that it would have been for reasons of state, not mere wilful wickedness: that a king had responsibilities to protect his crown, defend his country and avert civil war. All of which is perfectly true. And Richard III did become aware, in October 1483, of a serious threat centred around his nephews.

Historians also usually point to a catalogue of mediaeval kings who liquidated their rivals. This is the viewpoint of most textbooks and encyclopaedias. But not all kings liquidated their rivals, so this on its own is not adequate to prove anything. Henry IV, when he seized the throne in 1399, did not kill the king's under-age heir, who outlived three reigns and died in his bed. So although I have never denied that Richard may indeed have done away with the princes for reasons of state, given no reliable evidence either way it is simply not sufficient to convict him on the basis of tradition or conjecture.

In this instance, the main argument in favour of the death of the princes is the undeniable fact that they disappeared. Which may mean that they were killed, but again does not constitute proof. It is alleged that they were never seen again, but this cannot be said with certainty. There were uprisings during Henry VII's reign in favour of young lads that history is pleased to call pretenders, but their identities were never definitively established (unless you believe forced confessions). Among those who died in their support was Sir William Stanley, the man who gained Henry his crown at Bosworth. Plus, as we have seen, even Thomas More and Polydore Vergil recorded doubts whether the princes had been killed by Richard III. There are myriads of possible fates that could have befallen them, including the possibility that they survived and preferred to live out their later lives in protective obscurity. So once again we must not assume that we know as much as we're led to believe we know.

This is where today's ready availability of sources is so valuable, because it is easy to access published versions of texts cited here with the minimum of effort. Hence the readers of this little book are not expected to take anything on trust, but are encouraged rather to research and consider all the alternatives for themselves.

If we look at this as one might view a case in a court-room, we have a combination of three facts entered into evidence which seem on the surface to be reliable. First, that the deposed boys represented a potential threat to Richard III. Second, that a rumour arose among the rebels in September 1483 which said they had met a violent end. And third, that they disappeared from extant written records. It will not be possible to represent every nuance of opinion, but we can at least examine some arguments that arise from these assertions.

First, the potential threat

To what extent was Richard's position threatened?
* In the summer of 1483, Richard was in an advantageous position. He was already king, reigning with general consent and international recognition, and enjoying popular acclaim during his progress around the country. Unlike Edward V, he had been crowned and anointed in the presence of God, with the nobility of the land renouncing their oaths to Edward and swearing allegiance to him.

* He had assumed the throne by due process, being petitioned to reign after Edward IV's offspring were set aside – while still living – on grounds of canon law. If he now had to resort to eliminating them, it would be flying in the face of everything that publicly underpinned his legitimacy. It would be equivalent to admitting they had a rightful claim to the throne after all.

What were the precise security implications?

* Richard was aware of dissident opinion and expected it: there had already been a few isolated incidents, and they led him to prepare for unrest. But in early September he was unaware of any cohesive opposition, or at least was insufficiently concerned to cut short his progress. Until late September he had not even heard of Buckingham's betrayal and rebellion. There is no evidence that he would have viewed the princes as an imminent threat to his security at this time.

* Henry Tudor was an unknown quantity to Richard and it seems likely he underestimated him as an adversary in 1483. Since on the surface Tudor gained nothing by supporting Edward V's restoration, there was no obvious reason to suspect he would link up with the Woodville-inspired rebellion. In fact Tudor's name did not feature in any of Richard's written orders or proclamations until after the rebellion was quashed and his involvement became known.

* Edward V and his brother were securely under his control at the Tower of London. There was scarcely a safer place in the whole of his kingdom. In contrast, by killing the boys he would have made instant heiresses (in the eyes of his opponents) of their five sisters in sanctuary, over whom he had very little control at all. Already there were plots to spirit the girls overseas, and a guard had been placed at Westminster Abbey to try to prevent this. But the Abbey was not the Tower, and it would have been foolhardy to kill their brothers while leaving them so accessible. This echoes the policy of Edward IV in preserving the deposed Henry VI alive and in his power – which he did for six years – because while Henry continued living (and similarly while the princes continued living) it prevented anyone else from taking on the role of pretender. It is significant that Henry Tudor stepped up as pretender only once the rumour was put out that the princes were dead.

What were the practicalities?

* To arrange their killing in secret, at a distance, while he was far away in Yorkshire, would have been extremely risky. The Tower of London was a bustling royal palace inhabited by several hundred regular staff, including a garrison, not to mention a sizeable daily supply chain coming in and out to provide for men and beasts. There

would be huge practical problems of access, manpower, disposal of bodies and personal effects ... above all, how could the whole process remain totally unremarked and unreported? It is clear that Richard knew nothing of any organized rebellion in mid September, so if the thought occurred to him that he should do away with them, why do it at this awkward time when there was no pressing urgency? If he felt any action was needed at this moment, his most obvious course was to make perfectly normal arrangements to get them moved elsewhere.

* In practical terms, Richard's position was not so insecure that urgent and risky action was required to eliminate his brother's sons, especially while he was so far away that he could neither control the process nor ensure the necessary secrecy.

Second, the rumour and theories surrounding it

If even the Crowland chronicle could not venture an opinion whether the rumour was true, perhaps more can be gained by considering how and why it came to be spread.

Theory A. Since rumour was a prevalent device of propaganda in mediaeval times, it has been suggested that this one was deliberately spread by Richard III himself, his objective being to deter attempts to supplant him.

* Looking at the wider picture, although he may have perceived little in the way of co-ordinated threat to his crown, nevertheless he well knew the greed and ambition that pervaded many of England's powerful magnates (as exemplified by Buckingham and Tudor). Had he been so rash as to spread word that Edward IV's sons had been removed from contention it would be no deterrence at all, in fact it would be tantamount to announcing the removal of obstacles in the path of anyone who considered himself qualified to make a bid for the throne.

* If he was such a canny operator as to think up a double-bluff like this, he would soon reject it – because any potential advantage from the leak would be more than undermined by presenting a priceless propaganda gift to his opponents, inviting them to brand him a child-murderer.

Theory B. The boys had indeed been killed, and some scandalized citizen had found out and spread the news.

* On the face of it, this seems the most likely scenario. But there is no evidence to support it. This information should have been dynamite and should have spread like wildfire. To those taking part in the rebellion, we know the rumour was devastating. Yet we find no mention of messengers being sent spurring to the capital to try to substantiate it, or indeed citizens thronging the streets of London demanding an explanation of the fate of the children in the Tower. If they were known to have been killed there, London should have been the epicentre of rumour, action and unrest. But Londoners did not join in the October uprising. And no London civic record or guild book written in 1483 even notes the rumour of their demise at this time, nor does any civic record outside of the localities where rebellion was brewing. The irresistible impression is that word of their death appears to have been circulated chiefly among the rebels and in areas where they were congregating.

* If the boys had really been killed and the news leaked out, given so many hundreds of folk residing in and daily passing through the Tower of London, why did not a single soul come forward to identify anything about their disappearance, when or where it happened, or what became of them or their bodies? Why was nothing said even when Henry Tudor made enquiries on taking the throne – when divulging such information would have been greatly to their advantage? (It is safe to assume that Henry applied plenty of incentives to talk, especially when pretenders came along calling themselves the missing princes.)

* We are led to suppose, mainly from commentaries in later centuries, that the killing of the princes was seen as a deed of monstrous infamy. Yet there are no records from Richard's own period that demonstrate this sense of outrage. There is little speculation about it, and those references that exist are few and low-key (see later). The Crowland chronicle's report of the rumour says nothing of censure about such an act, whereas the killing of an abbey guard-dog merits an accusation of 'great inhumanity'. Even in the years after Richard's death it is only the self-styled chroniclers of history who set out to condemn their death as a particularly wicked murder.

A comparison may be instructive here. If we look at a note made by a London citizen in a record-book of around 1487, quite well into Henry VII's reign, he merely states succinctly and undramatically what everyone by now believes: the sons of Edward IV 'were put to death in the Tower of London'. Now compare this with the overheated words of his 20th-century editor, who describes their alleged death as 'this notorious act of political expediency'. Such a subjective outburst is even more surprising in the light of this editor's own caveat that his London citizen's notes 'can depend on nothing more than hearsay ... and current gossip (or perhaps propaganda)'. This is why every precaution must be taken to view the case in the light of the norms of those days, not our own.

Theory C. Persons unknown deliberately perpetrated the rumour to suit their own agenda.

* This sits well with the mention of the rumour's appearance at a particular time and in a particular context – among the rebels who would be the most affected by it – and occurring at a strategic moment when it was too late for them to turn back.

* It was especially useful to cast a slur on Richard III when he was in York, the farthest place from London in his entire itinerary. This meant it would take a long time to reach his ears, his options for publicly denying it were limited, and any such denials would have minimal impact in the south.

* It was spread among the very people who, in an effort to overthrow the king, were by now committed to treason. The rest of England, if they heard it, might ignore or disbelieve such a rumour, but these men could not afford to.

* *Qui bono?* Did someone benefit directly from it? It scarcely benefited the pro-Woodville rebels, as it destroyed the very cause they supported. By contrast, the reaction produced by the rumour was something earnestly desired by the family and promoters of Henry Tudor. Until now Tudor had been a little-known exile from a Lancastrian bloodline of questionable legitimacy. But the deaths of the princes would make their elder sister, Elizabeth of York, their heir in the eyes of the rebels, and nothing could be easier than for Tudor to promise a dynastic marriage with her, catapulting himself to the fore as their new candidate for king.

* For this to succeed he would need to be first in the know, and thus at the head of the queue to make an offer for Elizabeth's hand. Sure enough, we find in the Tudor records that Margaret Beaufort, his mother, hastens to put this very proposal to Elizabeth's mother the moment the rumour surfaces.

In summary, this combination of factors suggests a carefully planned scheme. Naturally there is no proof of this, and the rumour may have been entirely true or entirely lacking in ulterior motive (although political rumours seldom are or were). Its great advantage was that to achieve its specific goal it was a foolproof plan. Being anonymous, it involved no risk; being spread at a critical moment, it afforded scarcely any time to be checked or verified; and being aimed at a finely-targeted audience, it could not fail to have the desired effect.

Third, the disappearance of the princes

This is the last of those three apparently reliable facts entered into evidence in our imaginary court-room. So what does it tell us? Presumably we can agree that it is possible for a person to disappear without having been killed, therefore the disappearance of the princes is not in itself sufficient evidence of their death.

To support the case for the prosecution, it is claimed that Richard III's subjects generally believed he was responsible for killing them. However, there is actually very little evidence of this. If the researcher looks for reliable back-up in English annals of around September-October 1483, all that can be found are brief entries in civic records in Colchester and Bristol. In Colchester the record book contains a passing mention of Edward V, apparently indicating that he is deceased, although the Latin is not clear. In Bristol the civic *Kalendar* is alone in recording that the princes were 'put to silence in the Tower of London', but with no further elaboration. With rebellion afoot, both Colchester and Bristol were important centres where rumours would have circulated.

Apart from this there is some gossip around this time reported by foreigners, who can scarcely be regarded as reliable informants. Then immediately after Richard's death we have the Crowland chronicle looking back at the events of 1483 and recording that there

Lady Margaret Beaufort, Countess of Richmond,
Henry Tudor's mother

arose a rumour that the princes had met a violent end – but with no word, from someone who was thoroughly hostile to Richard, either confirming their death or condemning him for perpetrating it. This, then, must be a disappointing tally for anyone seeking signs of that general belief among Englishmen in their death and in Richard's guilt. Since history has characterized this as such a loathsome act, why wasn't there *some* reasonably well-informed source that cried out in condemnation?

On the other hand, it is known that the pockets of rebellion were localized in just a few areas, while the vast majority of the English population was uninvolved in the ambitions of the Woodvilles and Tudors. Richard's accession and rule had been promoted by the nobility and seems to have met with no popular dissatisfaction, nor did the uprising have any connection with Draconian laws, heavy taxes, religious persecution or other such oppressions.

Maybe the generality of Richard's subjects were aware that he had been forced to defend his crown against people who had the purely self-interested aim of replacing him with a child-king who would be under their control … and maybe their memories stretched back to the dark consequences of the last child-ruler. Perhaps there was less concern for the princes than we have been led to believe.

Later, encouraged by the Tudors on the throne, comments on their death naturally grew more accusatory, becoming positively histrionic when written for public consumption and to curry favour with the ruling party. The result was that the legend of the tragic princes eventually took on a mythical life of its own.

Even after Henry VII (or Thomas More) put out the story about James Tyrell having them smothered in their beds, many writers either doubted whether it ever happened, or ignored the authorized version and invented flights of fancy about a variety of different fates for them – some said they were locked in a chest and buried alive, some that they were drowned 'in the black deeps', and one story had the younger prince escaping to take shelter under the bed, but being caught at once and having his throat cut. These grisly imaginings have largely overtaken the reality of what might have been their real fate, which we will consider later.

Some fallacies and misconceptions

Misconceptions about dates.

Thanks mainly to Thomas More, it is widely assumed that the princes disappeared and were rumoured dead much earlier in the summer. It is more logical to assume that their actual disappearance or removal from the Tower of London coincided with the rumour, and the date of this can be verified by comparing dates of parallel events reported in the Crowland chronicle and elsewhere. From these indications it probably happened some time between about 10 and 20 September. Crowland is specific that it was not until after Buckingham had issued his proclamation as leader of the rebels that the rumour of their death was spread; and this proclamation could not have been earlier than about 10 September, otherwise Richard III would not have been still authorizing payments to him on 16 September.

The marriage of great convenience.
If we consult Tudor-era sources, we hear from Thomas More that it was his late patron Bishop Morton who conceived the idea of a marriage uniting Lancaster, in the person of Henry Tudor, and York in the person of the princes' sister Elizabeth, and persuaded the Duke of Buckingham to support it. Yet from Polydore Vergil we get the story that Henry's mother, Margaret Beaufort, had already agreed this deal with the queen mother, Elizabeth Woodville, in August – *before* Buckingham was suborned by Morton. Such an early date is highly unlikely. But Vergil was the official historian, with access to the highest ranks of Tudor informants, so evidently it's what his political masters wanted people to believe. Essentially they were peddling the story that Margaret had brought everyone together in coalition behind Henry and the marriage settlement – Morton, Buckingham, the Woodvilles and all the other rebels.

Because other commentators have failed to analyse these dates, and the circumstances around them, they have been content to believe that by the time the marriage was discussed, the Woodvilles had abandoned the princes in the belief that they were dead.

But if the two mothers were in talks this early, what they were really discussing was more likely a pact of assistance from Tudor's party in restoring Edward V. The hand of a princess could have been part of his reward once they had got Edward back on the throne. It simply doesn't make sense for the queen mother to give up on her boys in August and hand over a ready-made opportunity to Henry Tudor to seize the crown for himself. In fact anyone familiar with human nature will doubt whether Elizabeth tied up such a marriage deal even in September, when the rumour of her sons' demise first circulated. Like all leading magnates of the period, she had long-established networks of agents to keep her well informed. A mother's instincts would ensure she spent weeks and months searching for proof, and cling to the smallest hope that suggested her boys might still be alive, not supinely accept their death and sign her daughter over to the ambitious Tudor.

Nevertheless, as soon as the rumour surfaced among the rebels, we are told they believed Henry would take Elizabeth of York in marriage and, through her, the throne of England. But why should the English rebels believe such airy promises by this unknown Lancastrian expatriate? What proof did they have that the proposed partners weren't already betrothed to others? Also, because they were related, any marriage would need important prior arrangements such as a dispensation from the pope. These matters were not cobbled together so quickly. The reality underlying this supposed marriage agreement was that it was not a done deal but a plausible political artifice, aimed at those who unthinkingly believed what they were told. Against all the odds the marriage did eventually take place in 1486, so this became the authorized version of the story. But it was far more dubious than the Tudor gloss it later received.

The bones in Westminster Abbey.
There are some human remains of children in an urn in Westminster Abbey, which were discovered at the Tower in 1674 and assumed to be the remains of the princes. This assumption was based on no evidence other than Thomas More's story, or at least part of his story, which stated that they were secretly buried at the foot of a staircase in the Tower of London. Other parts of the same story – that they were later dug up by a priest and buried in a more suitable place, or possibly thrown into the Thames – were conveniently forgotten.

The original record of the discovery described the remains as 'two striplings in (as it seemed) a wooden chest', and they were found buried ten feet deep, at foundation level, under a stone staircase attached to the exterior of the White Tower (see illustration). They were initially thrown on to a rubbish heap until someone thought to take a second look. Typical later embellishments

*The Tower of London – entrance to the White Tower as it
may have looked in the 14th century – artist's impression of the
stone staircase where the remains of children were found in 1674*

added circumstantial details, e.g. that they were found 'face to face in a coffin', or that 'pieces of rag and velvet' were found with them, both assertions being impossible for the authors to have known owing to their sojourn amid the rubbish before retrieval. When the urn was opened and its contents thoroughly examined in 1933, there were no textiles or timber remnants present.

A great deal of faith has been placed in these remains as proof that Edward V and his brother met their death in the Tower of London, but nothing has ever established this. The depth at which they were found should immediately flag up doubts. In 1674 it took several workmen many days to remove the stone staircase above the discovery site and then excavate down to foundation level, so the idea that the boys were secretly buried here in 1483 does not hold water. It has yet to be explained, too, how the dismantling of a staircase and the excavation of a grave to an extraordinary depth of ten feet could possibly have taken place, in secret, right next to the one and only entrance of the White Tower at that time, a place of incessant traffic.

If we disregard these practical problems and look for confirmation in the bones themselves, unfortunately there was no way that the examination carried out in 1933 could have ascertained their antiquity, their gender, or even their ages. Science simply had not progressed that far. So until another attempt is made to identify them, perhaps using the more reliable evidence supplied by DNA, these boys or girls must remain anonymous.

In fact, if you make a rough calculation based on surface deposit accumulation, a possible year of burial could be 1066, when that particular spot was virgin ground. Another child's skeleton found at the Tower has been convincingly dated to the late Iron Age.

Rebellion to avenge the princes.
A misleading assertion, frequently encountered, is that the rebellion of 1483 was mounted 'in revulsion at the murder of the princes'. Nothing could be further from how it is characterized in the Crowland chronicle, the main source which describes the rebellion's development and progress in detail. This clearly states that it started as a movement to 'release them from captivity' and return the kingdom to its 'rightful heirs', which self-evidently assumes they

80

were still living. There was also a fallback plan to move their sisters abroad 'if any fate were to befall the male children', but no such fate is reported. Similarly a historian recently stated on the radio that revulsion about the princes caused forces to desert Richard III at Bosworth, but this is sheer conjecture – again there is no record of it. What is known for sure about Richard's betrayal at Bosworth is that it was a deliberate strategy by supporters of Henry Tudor and his family who wished to see Tudor on the throne.

Could some other person have killed the princes?

Of course it is not impossible that some other person might have killed the princes without Richard's knowledge, and the suggestion is not new. But it suffers from the same problems that beset the idea of *any* such act being carried out in secret at the busy Tower of London. Since their murderer would have been sentenced to certain death if discovered, and a particularly unpleasant death at that, it would have been crucial to preserve absolute secrecy at all costs. But how did you gain secret access, and how did you commit the deed and remove the bodies secretly in the middle of a royal residence?

Without this total secrecy it would not have remained an unsolved mystery to this day – there would have been witnesses and observers all over the grounds who would recollect such an abrupt and sensational disappearance. Tongues would wag about their unexplained absence from their religious observances and lessons, and how their apartments were occupied one day and suddenly empty the next, with servants and attendants wondering what their next duties were, and loose ends lying around everywhere.

For example, there would be no chance to remove their remaining books, playthings, clothing and other possessions in daily use, many of them no doubt costly and adorned with gems. With two boys, there would have been two sets of everything as befitted each one's age and stature. The nobility lived at close quarters with their attendants in those days, so the story of their unexpected disappearance, leaving all this behind, would have circulated within hours among all the residents of the Tower and the people who daily supplied it. Yet Henry VII found no one there who could enlighten him as to what happened to them, and it was not until 1502 (at the earliest) that the story of their death was apparently circulated.

My own conclusion is that they never were killed at the Tower, by Richard or by anyone else. Too many people would have known and remembered. They simply packed up and left as part of a preplanned departure for some alternative location, which all parties would have been expecting because their presence in London had become untenable.

An undramatic departure would have been completely normal, unremarkable and unmemorable, their destination known only to that small group who accompanied them, a group sworn to silence who, despite the Tudor king's demands, kept their word ever after. This continued silence speaks not of fear – for fear would have evaporated at Richard III's death – but of loyalty and of care for the safety of their charges.

So if we must investigate the possibility of some unknown person killing the princes, the likelihood is that it would have happened after they left the Tower. Someone who had efficient informants and plenty of finances could have learned the details of their departure and planned an ambush or assassination.

Who might have arranged this is a matter of pure speculation. Two candidates stand out as most likely, the first being the ungrateful Duke of Buckingham who turned against Richard and seems to have made a play for the crown himself. He had motive enough, if he wished to clear his own path to the throne, and having been recently appointed High Constable of England, he had the opportunity to make himself familiar with the Tower, its garrison, its facilities and its means of exit.

In the course of my researches I have ruled out Buckingham, even though suspicion seems to have attached itself to him from a very early date. No one has ever considered Buckingham a clever operator, in fact he is generally viewed as the dupe of that arch-schemer, Bishop John Morton, who persuaded him to abandon his trusted position at the side of Richard III and throw away his life to lead a risky rebellion.

A major problem with Buckingham is that it is difficult to believe he was in London after the month of July 1483 – the reports and evidences of his movements indicate that he was on his estates during August, and from there proceeded to join the rebel movement in early September.

Presenting himself as leader of the rebellion would have been a tricky job for one who currently enjoyed the title of Richard's High Constable, and would have involved a considerable amount of travelling between pockets of rebellion to persuade the various captains to accept his bona fides. To arrange an ambush or murder at long distance, while fully engaged in taking on the role of rebel leader, seems an unlikely achievement for someone without a history of intrigue. However, there is no conclusive evidence of Buckingham's whereabouts, so the suggestion is not altogether impossible.

A consideration not to be overlooked is that the one person who actually profited from the rumour of the death of the princes was Henry Tudor. If his faction were to press home their advantage, they could not afford for it to be proved false. From that moment and throughout all the years afterwards, while Tudor challenged and invaded and won the English crown, tussled with pretenders, and strove to convince the world that he sat securely on the throne, his entire position hinged upon the princes being dead.

He had to act in accordance with this stance, and he had to encourage this belief among everyone else – not least because one of his first actions was to repeal the 1484 Act of Parliament which had decreed the illegitimacy of the offspring of Edward IV. This repeal had the effect of legitimating Henry's bride to be, but simultaneously performed the same service for her brothers, who then automatically became Henry's rivals for the crown of England. So he insisted that the Act must be repealed without being read and every copy be destroyed on pain of condign punishment. This and other indications during his reign displayed a continued personal uncertainty regarding the possibly undead princes, which gave every impression that Henry was in genuine doubt as to their fate.

If any fingers are to be pointed in Henry Tudor's direction, logically accusations should centre around his wealthy family and supporters who were in England working assiduously in his interests during Richard's reign. They already included some of the major schemers and fixers of the age, who would prosper mightily during his coming reign and had no problem putting into practice the Tudor king's oppressive measures. If the killing of the princes had been organized by his family's enforcers, it would probably have been kept from the obsessively pious Henry; and he would have taken care not to ask awkward questions.

Does anything suggest the princes weren't killed?

Although Richard III has been in the dock for centuries, the only indication of any specific allegation against him seems to have been that put out after the supposed confession of James Tyrell in 1502. But neither the official allegation nor the confession exists in writing, so it is impossible to prove anything at this distance in time, unless new evidence is uncovered of course.

By the same token, it is impossible to bring any proof to counter it. It is a waste of effort to try to disentangle the theatrical web woven by Thomas More around whatever genuine facts may reside in his satirical drama, in which he presumes to give verbatim reports of Richard's conversations while seated 'at the draught'.

But there is significance to be found in some historical factors associated with the case, showing that the behaviour of the principal players was not quite what one would have expected if the princes had been put to death (or at least if Richard had been responsible).

Richard's actions.
Not only is evidence for the prosecution lacking, but Richard's actions do not support the assumption that he killed his nephews. For Richard III there was no profit unless it achieved what it's assumed he wanted – an end to Woodville attempts to restore their line. To achieve this once and for all there was one important action needed, and that was publicly to display their bodies in the time-honoured fashion, as when any prince died; claiming, of course, that their deaths arose from natural causes. Publicity would be essential, to prove convincingly to the world that they were no longer able to threaten him. But this was never done. Nor did he make any announcement of the princes' death, or seek to make it public by laying the blame on some other party. So if this was supposedly his motive for killing his nephews, his actions by cloaking it in secrecy entirely defeated his objective. Plus it should not be forgotten that Richard had other nephews and nieces, and made arrangements to

84

care for all of them. One nephew who might have posed a threat (to both Richard and Henry Tudor) was the orphaned eight-year-old Earl of Warwick. Under Henry VII he was imprisoned and executed.

The promotion of their sisters.
Actually, it has yet to be shown what benefit Richard *did* achieve by allegedly killing the princes, since the effect their disappearance had in reality was to clear the way for Henry Tudor to take on the role of pretender.

Richard, like all men who had to lead armies, doubtless avidly studied the game of chess along with his books on military strategy. There is in chess a phenomenon known as promotion, whereby a pawn may be transformed to the rank of a queen. Richard knew well that if the boys were eliminated, then each of their five sisters was automatically promoted to the rank of potential queen – and the floodgates would immediately be opened for any pretender to try his luck on the promise of marrying one of them. By contrast, while the princes were living in his custody he held complete power over the entire Woodville line of succession, because their party would never promote a daughter in preference to Edward IV's sons. It is highly significant that Richard made no move to seize the sisters, which he certainly would have done if he had been planning to kill their brothers.

Elizabeth Woodville's behaviour.
The Tudor myth is that Elizabeth Woodville immediately fell into lamentations on hearing of the death of her sons, and made a pact with Henry Tudor's mother that gave him the succession in right of her eldest daughter. This, as previously observed, is contradictory to the reaction one would expect of the doughty queen-mother, who with her ample resources would have spared no efforts to ascertain their fate. The rebellion currently in progress was aimed at restoring Edward V, so it would be ridiculous to give up on him so quickly. It was the Tudor party that was in desperate haste to promote Henry Tudor to the role of contender for the crown – but his ambitions ran contrary to the interests of her sons.

So we can take it as certain that Elizabeth would have continued strenuous investigations into their disappearance. Nevertheless, by late February she reached an agreement with Richard to cease her stay in sanctuary. What is more, she placed all her daughters into Richard's care and he undertook to find honourable husbands for them, a promise he was arranging to fulfil when he was killed. Had she believed the princes were dead, this would have been unthinkable because the princesses would by then have become her only remaining bargaining counter: giving them into Richard's power would have meant giving away her one trump card.

Elizabeth also contacted her eldest son by her previous marriage, who had joined Tudor in Brittany, urging him to return and make his peace (Tudor's men stopped him). This should be sufficient to dispel any supposition that her agreement with Richard was made under duress.

There are other aspects of her later behaviour in the reign of Henry VII that defy conventional explanation, including the absence of any accusation against Richard. Many writers have contorted themselves trying to rationalize Elizabeth Woodville's reconciliation with the king who supposedly killed her sons, whereas her actions become straightforward if seen in the light of Richard's innocence.

No recorded accusations by Henry Tudor.
Equally significant is the lack of any known murder accusation by Henry Tudor as he marched through England before and after the battle of Bosworth, when he sorely needed arguments to bolster his challenge for the crown. No written record exists of Henry VII ever directly accusing Richard – not in proclamations, and not even in the Act of Attainder at his first Parliament where Richard III and the entire royal army at Bosworth were pronounced guilty of treason against 'King' Henry. There is one section in the attainder which contains a list of Richard's supposed misdeeds including 'shedding of infants' blood', a vague and inadequate phrase if we are supposed to think that it refers to the crime of 'regicide – an accusation which the Tudors had ensured was already being spread by rumour – unless, of course, it actually *was* no more than rumour.

Henry VII was quite happy for others to make accusations, but despite his well known piety he never called for any requiem mass or commemoration for the princes, or at least none is recorded, even when (or if) he supposedly obtained proof of their death with the

Tyrell confession. Presumably their mother provided him with no useful intelligence either. This at the very least suggests there was a complete absence of convincing evidence. And we can be absolutely certain that evidence was avidly sought throughout Henry's reign – especially when pretenders kept popping up – and even more so when he needed to provide other European royal houses with assurances that his fledgling dynasty wouldn't be overthrown by one of the missing princes returning to claim his kingdom.

The Portuguese marriage.
Once again this little book is prevented by lack of space from including many interesting issues which were explored at length in *Richard III: The Maligned King*. One of these was Richard III's marriage treaty with the Portuguese royal family after the death of his wife, Queen Anne. With this marriage, and without spilling a single drop of blood, Richard would have achieved a union between the royal houses of York and Lancaster in the persons of himself and Princess Joanna of Portugal, she being the senior living (and eligible) female descendant of the line of Lancaster. At the same time the treaty would have fulfilled his promise of finding an honourable husband for the eldest sister of the princes, in the person of the young Duke of Beja, a marriage which coincidentally would have seen her, in a few years time, as queen of Portugal.

Although all this was prevented by his death at Bosworth, the significance of this treaty should not be overlooked. It showed that Richard was held in the highest esteem by the Portuguese, and in particular by the very devout Princess Joanna, known to this day as The Holy Princess who, having refused all other suitors, was unlikely to consent to such a marriage alliance had she heard that he was believed to be a tyrant and murderer.

What if the princes disappeared and survived?

There are innumerable possibilities of what might have happened in the future life of either prince if he survived. In a grown-up world where we accept Big Bang theories and Dark Matter, it should not be impossible for us to accept that some questions from past centuries are destined to remain unanswered.

The Water Gate on the River Thames at the Tower of London

Actually, disappearances from the historical record are nothing unusual. People are exercised about the disappearance of the 'Princes in the Tower' precisely because they were princes. No such fuss has been made about the little sons of the Earl of Desmond, who were said to have been killed in the reign of Edward IV at the behest of his queen; or about the missing infant offspring of 'Perkin Warbeck' (see later) who disappeared when their father was executed by Henry VII. Their deaths, if they were killed, would have been no less tragic, and their killers would have had no such reasons of state as prevailed in October 1483, when Edward V and his brother had been placed at the head of an active rebellion.

Because the missing princes have been accepted as pathetic victims in dramatic literature, little thought has been given to other possible outcomes for them, still less to the logistics involved.

Whatever their ultimate fate, the odds are that Richard never intended the two young boys to remain in such an unsuitable place as the Tower of London for any length of time. In any case it would be foolhardy to leave them in such a central and exposed location. Probably in July, after his coronation, he would have sent an ultimatum to the Woodville party letting them know the terms under which he was prepared to reconcile and receive them back in favour. Since they were scattered, he would appreciate that their response would not be quick. Communications would also be further delayed by his progress around the country.

It might not have been until his arrival in York at the end of August that he became convinced his overtures had been ignored and the Woodville threat was now active. Clearly he was unaware of how far their tentacles had reached, but removing the princes from the capital was an elementary precaution, and it could have been now that he started to make arrangements. With the Tower having a Water Gate straight out on to the River Thames, this was the obvious route for conveying them away.

They could have been bound for a destination in England, but more likely a refuge overseas would have been preferred, quite possibly in Flanders or elsewhere in the Low Countries where the house of York had long-standing ties, and where members of their family had taken cover in dangerous times in the past. Their aunt, Richard's sister Margaret, had long enjoyed an exalted position as Duchess of Burgundy, and with her lands and connections she was more than capable of finding means of sequestering the boys. Since Richard himself had a small son of about the same age, there can be little doubt that he would have contacted Margaret making plans for refuge for his own boy if the worst came to the worst. The same plans could easily have embraced the sons of Edward IV.

England was nowhere near so insular in those days as might be supposed – in fact, a hiding-place overseas was proposed by the 1483 rebels for the sisters of Edward V. The Continent was easily accessible, especially to someone like Richard who owned ships and had strong maritime connections, as did his able lieutenant, the Duke of Norfolk, who was residing near Ipswich at this time and acting as the king's eyes and ears in the south.

Since the pretender known as 'Perkin Warbeck' has now been mentioned – or as Henry VII dubbed him, 'Piers Osbeck' – we cannot avoid the fact that he was enthusiastically promoted by Duchess Margaret in his campaign in the 1490s against the Tudor king. Many people, including Henry, believed he had been trained by her. Several European crowned heads accepted him as Richard of York, the younger of the two princes, returning to claim his crown after growing up in Flanders. He was ultimately unsuccessful, but his efforts were supported by thousands of men from England and other countries who were prepared to fight and die in his cause.

Historians have generally reached the conclusion that he was an impostor because after capture he was forced to sign a confession to this effect; but who can trust confessions wrung by the Tudors from their captives under duress? His identity remains yet another mystery and incapable of being proved either way unless new evidence comes to light. The best account of his life has been written by Ann Wroe under the title *Perkin: A Story of Deception.*

These are just a very few illustrations of possible outcomes that have been suggested for Edward V and his brother. It's easy to forget that Richard III had every reason to look forward to a long and prosperous reign; but he also needed to be prepared in case he was challenged by pretenders – a good reason for keeping the genuine princes safely in hiding so he could produce them as a last resort.

On the other hand, once having left London, they could have suffered any number of mishaps en route to any destination, including a shipwreck or piracy at sea. For their own safety it would be necessary for the boys to be separated (they had lived separately their whole lives), so the fate of one is not necessarily bound up with that of the other. It's impossible to know whether one or both boys might have died as youths or adults, from natural or other causes. In those times of high infant mortality it was not at all unusual for children, even royal children, to die at an early age despite the best possible care. Richard's little son died in 1484, and even Henry VII's eldest son, Arthur Tudor, died in 1502 at the age of 15.

*'Perkin Warbeck' or 'Piers Osbeck' or 'Richard IV' –
was he the missing prince Richard of York?*

Who was ultimately responsible for the fate of the princes?

Many commentators have said that if the boys met an untimely end,
Richard III must be held responsible because they were in his care.
Actually, the realities of the times meant that a protector was
primarily Lord Protector of the Realm, not of his brother's
illegitimate children. Equally, when Richard came to the throne as

King of England, his first responsibility was to preserve and protect his crown and people. Meanwhile the princes were being used as figureheads in a tussle to regain the crown by their family and supporters – whose schemes, had they triumphed, would have resulted in Richard's defeat and death. He had been summoned to ascend the throne at the demand of those representatives of Parliament who, having considered the problem of the succession, had rejected being ruled by children of questionable parentage. As king, it was not part of his role to sacrifice himself for their sake.

We cannot know what the princes thought of waging war on their uncle. Children were, and remained for many centuries, mere pawns in the hands of their families. But these were not ordinary children. It may not make for comfortable reading, but if Edward V considered himself old enough to be the crowned and anointed ruler of England, he was old enough to understand that intrinsic to this role was a king's task to defend and fight for his crown, perhaps dying in the process.

If he did actually share his family's ambitions to reclaim the throne, then he was placing himself at the head of a rebellion, and he knew precisely the significance of that. Only a dozen years previously the last Prince of Wales before him, Edward of Lancaster, had been spurred on by his mother to lead an army against the reigning king, and had been cut down on the battlefield at the age of seventeen.

A child of twelve might have thought himself capable of many ambitions beyond his years, but if it was anyone's job to protect that child it was his mother and her family and supporters who were making decisions which would determine his fate.

Comparing the case of the young Mortimer heir apparent to the throne in 1399 – the boy from Richard's ancestry who was removed from the succession by Henry IV – this lad's family reached an accommodation with the king who had deprived him of the crown. The Woodville party, being on the losing side in 1483, could similarly have made their peace and reconciled with the new regime. It was quite normal for royalty and the nobility to receive pardons. In fact even after Richard had been forced to put down the uprising in October, he was still ready to pardon and reconcile with the Woodvilles and other leading rebels.

Logically, then, they must have considered the option of accommodating with Richard and rejected it. In this context there arises a very significant question. How did they justify placing the princes in such a hazardous position, i.e. heading up a rebellion against the king, while the boys were completely powerless and completely under his control?

You might think they did so because, having known Richard for nearly twenty years, his in-laws felt they knew a thing or two about his character. But if they had any vestige of doubt as to whether they could safely predict his behaviour (and bearing in mind that by the time he was crowned he had executed two members of their family and a couple of their supporters), weren't they taking a massive gamble playing this game of power with two young lives? At what point might a king find that the exigencies of stamping out rebellion outweighed whatever personal scruples he had?

For people who see Richard only through the veil of his black legend, it may be difficult to accept that if he did put the princes to death it would have been an action forced upon him. A fifteenth-century king's decisions were not those of an ordinary man, and he did not have the luxury of sitting inactive and allowing civil war to tear England apart.

Conclusion

Ultimately, when weighing up the Great Debate about Richard III, his actions cannot be separated from the turbulent events of his time.

* First there was the succession crisis caused by the revelation that the late king's secret marriages had bastardized his children, which wiped out confidence in the princes as being fit to rule England.

* Second there was Richard's acceptance of the heavy burden of sovereignty, and his need to hold the realm steady and united under his leadership.

* Third there was the threat of the Woodvilles, who might have reconciled with Richard but decided not to.

* This left him with his dilemma over the sons of Edward IV, whom he would have wished to keep safe, but whose family and

supporters had decided to make them the focus for rebellion. What was the right thing to do in these circumstances?

We have considered a little of what happened in the year 1483, but nothing of Richard III's two-year rule in a general sense, which in many ways was progressive and enlightened, with a major emphasis on justice for both rich and poor. He was recognized as an intelligent and courageous man. Above all he was a man of his time, and a king of his time.

I hope this introduction to the Great Debate has encouraged readers to want to find out more for themselves. It is only in the exercise of our own intelligence that we can distinguish facts from biased opinions, rational judgements from facile traditions ... and, hopefully, separate dramatic fiction from something far more interesting and challenging: the study of real history.

INDEX